About Policy Exchange

Policy Exchange is an independent think tank whose mission is to develop and promote new policy ideas which will foster a free society based on strong communities, personal freedom, limited government, national self-confidence and an enterprise culture.

Policy Exchange is committed to an evidence-based approach to policy development. We work in partnership with academics and other experts and commission major studies involving thorough empirical research of alternative policy outcomes. We believe that the policy experience of other countries offers important lessons for government in the UK. We also believe that government has much to learn from business and the voluntary sector.

Lion Cubs?

Lessons from Africa's Success Stories

Edited by Anna Reid

Introduction by David Cowan

Research and charts by Jamey Borell

First published in January 2004 by Policy Exchange

Policy Exchange
Clutha House
10 Storey's Gate
London SW1P 3AY
Tel: 020 7340 2650
www.policyexchange.org.uk

ISBN 0 9545611 4 7
Typeset by Politico's Design, design@politicos.co.uk

Contents

About the Authors

Brian Cooksey (tadreg@raha.com) is founder and director of the Tanzanian Development Research Group, based in Dar es Salaam. He holds a Phd in Sociology from the University of Birmingham, and writes on a range of development-related topics. Recent publications include 'Aid and Corruption in Africa' EIU, Sub-Saharan Africa: Regional Overview, 2003; 'Marketing Reform? The Rise and Fall of Agricultural Liberalisation in Tanzania' Development Policy Review, 21 (1): 67-90, 2003; and 'The Power and the Vainglory: Anatomy of a Malaysian IPP in Tanzania', in K.S. Jomo ed *Ugly Malaysians? South-South Investments Abused*, Centre for Black Research, Durban 2002.

David Cowan is Senior Economist at the Economist Intelligence Unit in London. He has a Phd from the University of London, which examined the impact of Tanzania's structural adjustment programmes from the mid-1980s to early '90s. He worked for six years as Principal Research Officer at the Bank of Botswana, and for three in the Economic Research Unit of the Saudi Arabian Ministry of Foreign Affairs.

Douglas Mason is Editor of the Economist Intelligence Unit's Africa department. He holds degrees from McGill University, the University of Cambridge, the University of East Anglia and the London School of Economics. He has worked as a development consultant in Mozambique, Sudan, Zimbabwe and South Africa, and participated in the UN peace-keeping operation in Mozambique from 1994-'99.

Gregory Mthembu-Salter covers Rwanda, Burundi, Democratic Republic of Congo and Zambia for the Economist Intelligence Unit. Based in Cape Town, he has studied Rwanda's and Burundi's peace-making processes for the city's Centre for Conflict Resolution, and Rwandan cross-border trade for the World Bank.

Ian Taylor is Senior Lecturer in Politics and International Relations at the University of Botswana. He holds a MPhil from the University of Hong Kong, and a DPhil from the University of Stellenbosch. He contributes to South African television and to the independent press in Zimbabwe. His most recent publication is Fredrik Soderbaum and Ian Taylor (eds) *Regionalism and Uneven Development in Southern Africa: the Case of the Maputo Development Corridor*, Aldershot: Ashgate 2003. *Africa in International Politics: External Involvement on the Continent*, edited with Paul Williams, will be published by Routledge in February 2004.

Editor's Summary

Contrary to what documentary-makers would have one believe, not every African country is riven by famine and civil war. Out of the headlines, several have been doing well, growing their economies and building stable, inclusive governments. How real are these successes? How were they achieved? And what can Western donors and other African governments learn from them?

Lion Cubs brings together four country case studies – of Tanzania, Botswana, Rwanda and Mozambique. They were chosen on the basis of their economic performance, but also all boast governments that are, if not Sweden-clean, at least stable and responsible. South Africa, though by far the richest country on the continent, was left out as constituting a special case that provides fewer lessons for others.

Viewed in close-up none of these countries are, of course, "utopias in the Kalahari". Tanzania has a long history of misusing aid; Botswana suffers one of the world's highest rates of HIV infection; the Tutsi-dominated Rwandan government suppresses legitimate Hutu discontents; Mozambique is dangerously split between richer south and poor north. Everywhere, the benefits of growth are unequally spread, and governments honour pluralism more in letter than in spirit. Nowhere have they grasped the nettle of stronger property-rights on land.

Their achievements are nonetheless real and replicable. Botswana's prudent management of its diamond reserves demonstrates that they need not prove the curse that they have for Angola and Sierra Leone. Its culture of clean government, Ian Taylor argues, stems partly from historical good luck, but also from rules preventing civil servants from entering politics, and from an active, high-profile Directorate on Corruption and Economic Crime. An unusual willingness to recruit Westerners into the civil service has strengthened economic planning and allowed skills transfer to local hires.

Tanzania, having finally achieved macro-economic stability, shows that privatisation works. Its container port and electricity provider have both improved their services dramatically since being sold or put out to private management contract. But as elsewhere, the government's failure properly to break up state-owned farm-goods monopsonies continues to exacerbate rural poverty. Tanzania also demonstrates the perils of long-term aid dependency: Brian Cooksey thinks that donors should be tougher and more consistent on conditionality, concentrating on outputs rather than processes, and insisting that basic reforms are achieved before moving on to the latest policy fad.

Rwanda, scene of some of the worst inter-communal violence of the twentieth century, provides a remarkable lesson in post-conflict state-building and economic recovery. By making peace with neighbours, accepting moderate Hutus into government, and bringing those involved in the 1994 massacres to trial as quickly as possible,

Rwanda seems gradually to be escaping the politics of race, as proven by Kagame's genuine popularity across ethnic lines. Greg Mthembu-Salter recommends that despite election-rigging, the IMF should continue to support the government, on the grounds that its poverty-reduction policy is sincere and sensible, and that if not made upfront and explicitly, political conditionality devalues demands for equally important economic reforms.

Mozambique also demonstrates that reconciliation is possible even after the bloodiest civil war. The UN's peacekeeping mission of '93-4 proved one of the organisation's most successful, disarming Renamo militiamen and providing them with the capital and equipment to return to their villages and start farming. Renamo leaders were wooed with a $19m "trust-fund". Having once been notorious for conscripting children and mutilating civilians, Renamo now forms a legitimate, peaceful political opposition. Similar approaches to militias elsewhere, Douglas Mason suggests, might be more successful than conventional peace-keeping.

All these achievements, David Cowan points out in his introduction, are occurring against the background of two under-reported but transformative developments: first, deregulation of and new investment in airlines and telecoms; second, oil finds in the Gulf of Guinea. Better communications reinforce initiatives to break down intra-African trade barriers, as well as bringing to an end an era when the quickest way to get from Lagos to Nairobi was via London or Paris. And Africa's new oil revenues, thanks to monitoring by NGOs and multilaterals, should be better spent than before. The regional powers – Cote d'Ivoire in the west, Kenya in the east, South Africa in the south – will be vital, he argues, in pulling along the smaller economies. By getting a few of the big countries right, donors can spread prosperity through a much wider area.

Post-apartheid talk of an "African Renaissance" turned out to be overblown. But as these papers show, the poorest and most divided societies can be turned around, given good policies and – harder – the will to put them into practice.

Introduction

David Cowan

In the mid-1990s there was much talk of political and economic renaissance in sub-Saharan African. Apartheid had ended in South Africa, and a wave of democracy seemed to be sweeping the continent. An article in the *Financial Times*[1] encapsulated the optimism in its title: 'Ripples of a revolution'. It argued that the exile of the Zairian dictator Mobuto Sese Seko was "reverberating across the continent", and that new leaders were emerging who would challenge economic orthodoxies, and supplant the *ancien régimes* of francophone Africa, Kenya and Zimbabwe. Chief amongst this coming generation were Yoweri Museveni in Uganda, Paul Kgame in Rwanda, Issayas Afeworki in newly-independent Eritrea and Meles Zenawi in Ethiopia. As importantly, political transformation seemed to be occurring against a background of genuine economic reform. In 1995 and 1996 sub-Saharan Africa as a whole posted economic growth rates of 3.8% and 4.6% respectively, compared to global growth rates of only 3.6% and 4.1%.

Nearly a decade later the situation seems much less bright, and talk of a new political and economic dawn is muted. Although there has been limited political progress in Kenya, with former president Daniel arap Moi voted out of office in December 2002, this has been offset by events elsewhere. Examples include ongoing political crisis in Zimbabwe and political implosion in Cote d'Ivoire, leading to civil war and the country's effective division in two. Moreover, although many former dictators have embraced the concept of democracy, they have yet to implement its spirit. Instead, they have simply taken on many of the formal elements of democracy, such as the holding of elections, but have become adept in ensuring that they and their parties win, by whatever means necessary. Even more worryingly, aid and new debt flows to the continent have slowed in recent years,[2] while it faces a huge humanitarian and economic crisis in the form of the HIV/AIDS pandemic. In a new report by UNAIDS, *Accelerating Action against AIDS in Africa*, the UN body estimated that by 2005 sub-Saharan Africa will require US$5bn to fund basic services to treat the pandemic, and US$1bn more to fund the provision of anti-retrovirals for 2.5m people. This is more that 10 times the amount spent in 2000, and double what is expected to be available.

Despite optimism at the time, in retrospect the '90s were a lost decade in terms of economic growth. Save for a few years in the middle of the decade, economic performance was poor. In the five years from 1990-'94, real GDP growth in sub-Saharan Africa averaged only 1.5% per annum. After rising for a couple of years in the mid-'90s, by 1999 it had fallen back to 2%. Africa, analysts began to worry, was slipping ever further behind the rest of the world, and turning into a continent of permanent under-development. As the IMF recently pointed out, even if sub-Saharan Africa were to grow at a real 3% per annum, it would still take 40 years to reach the current average income level of other developing countries.

The academic literature on the causes of Africa's poor economic performance is plentiful and depressing. Although not an exhaustive list, the following give an indication of the scale of the problems that have to be overcome.

Most basically of all, many economists argue, sub-Saharan Africa has been dealt a poor hand by nature. Its combination of climate and geography means that its soils are fragile, and, despite often lush vegetation, largely unsuitable for intensive farming. The climate is also conducive to diseases, including malaria, yellow fever and sleeping sickness. In 1997 a study by the Harvard Institute for International Development concluded that these constraints put sub-Saharan Africa at a permanent disadvantage; in fact, if the equation uses to estimate growth by HIID is interpreted literally, incomes in tropical countries will only in the long term ever reach just over half those in temperate climes.

To this must be added a host of other handicaps. Colonial rule left sub-Saharan Africa with little infrastructural development outside a few major cities, and clumsily-drawn national borders that encourage ethnic conflict. In most countries, the structure of land ownership is tribal, meaning that individuals do not have the clearly-defined property rights that would incentivise them to improve their land, or allow them to borrow against it. Dependence on commodity exports puts governments at the mercy of fluctuating world commodity prices. And notoriously, sub-Saharan Africa has been poorly served by its political leaders, more than a fair share of whom – from Mobuto in Zaire to Amin in Uganda and Bokassa in the Central African Republic – are best forgotten.

A Low Base

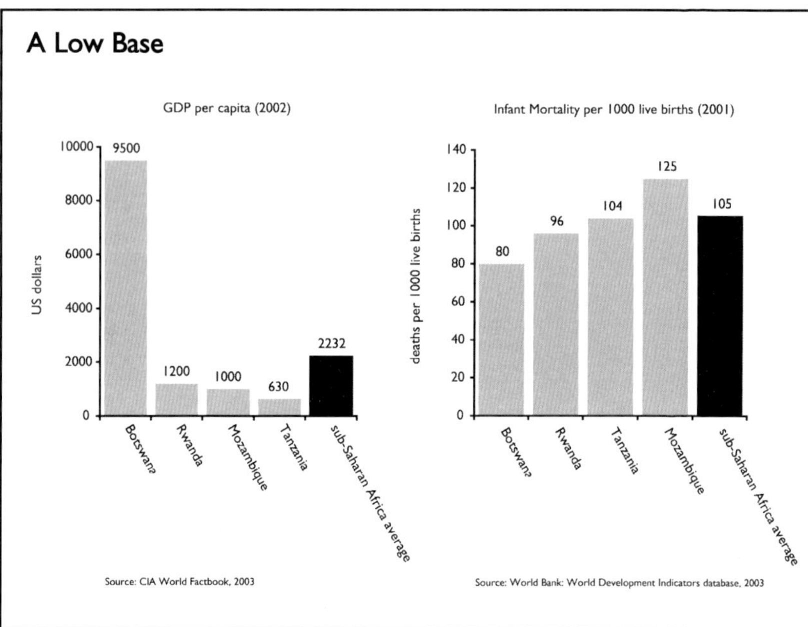

Following a lost decade in terms of economic growth, and faced with this litany of constraints to development, it is not surprising that, for many, the outlook is bleak. However, this does not mean that it is without hope. First, although some countries have gone backwards rapidly – notably Zimbabwe, Kenya and Cote d'Ivoire – others have gone forward. Ghana managed a peaceful democratic transition from military rule under Jerry Rawlings to civilian rule under former opposition leader John Kufour, and has continued to grow its economy. Senegal has made a similar transition from one-party to multi-party government, also against a background of economic growth. Democracy in Mozambique, Tanzania and Uganda may be more fragile, but all three nonetheless exhibit a degree of political pluralism, and have performed well in terms of economic reform and growth. Botswana and Mauritius have grown rapidly, despite little attention from international media. Finally the outlook for the sub-continent's two largest economies is far from hopeless: South Africa continues to make steady progress following its political transition, and Nigeria has managed to achieve reasonable economic growth since its return to civilian rule in 1999 (although largely oil-driven, and from a low base.) Forecasters are now cautiously optimistic about the continent as a whole, estimating annual growth rates of 3%-5% over the next few years.

Their optimism is well founded, thanks to two crucial but under-reported transformations currently underway in Africa. First, although the end of apartheid has not yet sparked wholesale political reform, it is driving an economic revolution that is clearly visible to anyone visiting today. In capital cities throughout the region, you can now buy South African products and eat in South African fast food chains, while watching South African satellite television. According to Liquid Africa, a South African brokerage and research group, South African companies have invested US$1.4bn a year in sub-Saharan Africa since 1991, while in 2002 around 20% of South Africa's total exports went to other sub-Saharan African countries. As well as high-profile investment in retail – which is often limited in terms of value although very visible – there has been substantial large scale, long-term investment in mines, railways and power.[3]

South African companies are also transforming how Africans communicate and travel. Two South African firms, MTN and Vodacom, have been at the forefront of bringing mobile telephony, and a communications revolution, to many sub-Saharan countries.[4] In a continent where state-owned telecommunications providers had overcharged and under-invested for decades, the mobile phone has been gratefully embraced, especially by hard-pressed businesses (both large and small). The airline industry is undergoing a similar shake-up. South African Airways has bought a majority share in formerly state-owned Air Tanzania and is looking to develop Dar-es-Salaam as an East African hub. If it also, as expected, buys a West African carrier – perhaps Ghana Airways or a reconstituted Nigerian Airways – this will give it three hubs from which to provide services across the continent, where in the past it was often cheaper and quicker to fly from Lagos to Nairobi via London or Paris.

In both these cases, South African investment is simultaneously encouraged by, and encouraging, reform. After decades of resistance, state-owned telecommunications companies are starting to be privatised, or turned over to private-sector management companies, partially in the knowledge that otherwise they will collapse in the face of competition from mobile. Most of these newly-privatised companies have ambitious targets to install landlines as part of their terms of sale, the first time in many decades that there has been substantial large-scale investment in telephone infrastructure. Similarly, while South African Airways builds a continent-wide network, so the closure of many national airlines has led to the emergence of more dynamic private airlines: Precision Air in Tanzania and Bellview Airlines in Nigeria are leading examples of these new carriers, which not only fly within their countries, but also to neighbouring ones.

For South African companies, sub-Saharan Africa is a crucial part of their long-term growth strategy. Few South African companies (with notable exceptions such as Anglo American, Investec and South African Breweries), can compete on a global scale, but they carry weight regionally, and have experience in operating in difficult business environments. In contrast, the African operations of most multinationals, although long established and often very profitable, represent only a tiny percentage of their total operations, and have little influence on wider strategic decision-making.

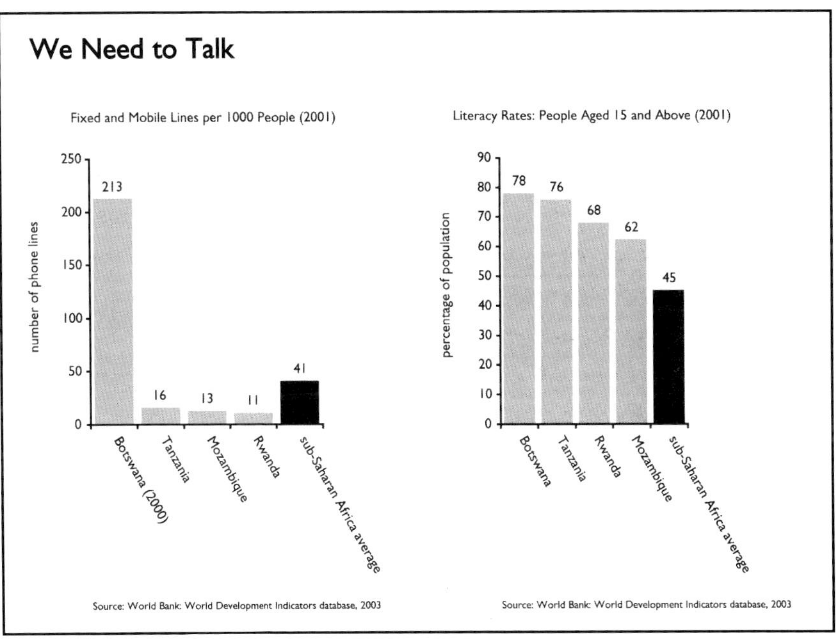

The second economic transformation underway is the development of the oil industry in the Gulf of Guinea. This has boosted the economies of a few small countries in spectacular fashion – Equatorial Guinea's real GDP grew by an astronomical 62.5% in 2001, and Chad's is forecast to grow by 58% in 2004 – but will also have wider, longer-term effects. The Economist Intelligence Unit estimates that total oil production from the Gulf of Guinea will increase from 3.7m barrels per day (b/d) in 2002, to 7.4m b/d in 2010. In the past, this windfall might have proven a curse rather than a blessing: African governments have a depressing history of wasting income from natural resources on illegal personal enrichment, warfare, and white-elephant development projects. As a study by Jeffery Sachs and Andrew Warner[5] confirms, in Africa an abundance of natural resources tends actually to depress rather than stimulate growth, partially because most countries do not have the political or economic institutions to manage them.

However, Equatorial Guinea's oil riches are arriving in a different global environment. While there remains huge scope for waste, the global community will at least monitor governments' use of resources far more closely. The rise of the internet and of non-governmental organisations (NGOs), means that even in the absence of effective domestic political opposition, governments – and perhaps more importantly, the multinational oil companies – are closely scrutinised. Even Nigeria, having squandered its oil wealth for decades, has announced that it will try to become involved in the Britain and World Bank-sponsored Extractive Industries Transparency Initiative. Together with similar initiatives such as "Publish What you Pay" (backed by 160 NGOs), this aims to force governments to reveal much more about financial flows from the mining and energy sectors than in the past.[6]

There are, therefore, good grounds for hope that a combination of South African investment and oil-led growth in West Africa will drive a new wave of economic growth around the continent. Moreover, this comes at a time when African elites are beginning to understand that poor economic policy is a major constraint to development. Although many argue that Botswana has little to teach other African countries given its small size, ethnic homogeneity and proximity to South Africa, this is a mistake. Botswana's real lessons for the rest of Africa are not the obvious, dramatic ones – such as that avoiding civil war is good for growth – but dull, technical ones about the careful use of economic planning and cost-benefit analysis to direct limited resources to where they will have most impact (education being key). Solid budgeting processes help the government to cope with volatile diamond prices, and its 50:50 shareholding split with De Beers in the national mining company ensures that De Beers' interests and its own remain closely aligned.

Even Botswana faces constraints. Small and landlocked, it depends on exports for growth. Transport costs mean that exporting to countries outside Southern Africa is difficult, so its best hope is that it can ride on the coat-tails of larger neighbours – South Africa, Zimbabwe and perhaps even the Democratic Republic of Congo and Angola. Botswana promotes the idea that it can be an international services centre, but despite its skilled workforce is likelier to succeed if surrounding countries grow strongly, encouraging investors to use Botswana as headquarters or back-office provider for their regional operations. Similar arguments can be put forward in West Africa, where smaller economies such as Burkina Faso and Mali need a helping hand from Côte d'Ivoire. In East Africa, Kenya could act as an engine of regional growth for inland Rwanda and Burundi. Asia's "flying geese formation" concept – the idea that development in one country helps drag along others – applies in Africa too.

Accordingly, one of the most disappointing developments of the 1990s was the collapse of three of Africa's most important economies. In the early 1990s Côte d'Ivoire, Kenya and Zimbabwe –

all relatively advanced, diversified and pluralist – were seen as positive examples. But by the mid to late '90s all were mired in deep political and economic crisis. This has dragged down growth in the entire continent, and for it to really pick up again the international community and other sub-Saharan African leaders need to help fashion long-term political solutions in all three countries.

African governments must also accept that globalisation is a force for good, not a threat. The fact that the collapse of the Cancun trade talks in September was welcomed by many African governments shows the extent to which these arguments have not been won. Instead, anti-globalisaton NGOs seem to have won the day.[7] This flies in the face both of the Asian development experience and of a huge body of academic research demonstrating that trade, especially in manufactured goods, is a key engine of economic growth.

In Africa's case, globalisation can hardly be the cause of its woes, since it never integrated with the global economy in the first place. The whole of sub-Saharan Africa accounts for less than 1% of world GDP, making its combined economy about the same size as that of the Netherlands. In 2000 world exports were US$6,369bn, compared to exports from sub-Saharan Africa of US$95 billion – around 1.5% of the world total. In an average year, sub-Saharan Africa attracts only 0.5% of total global foreign investment inflows. The only sub-Saharan African country, apart from South Africa, which has really sought to integrate with the global economy – Mauritius – has an economic record that is the envy of most other countries on the continent.

Similarly, African countries trade surprisingly little with each other. Their external links tend still to be with ex-colonial powers rather than with neighbours. Even when they display apparent commitment to boosting intra-African trade – through the East African Community or the Southern African Development Community – it often proves rhetorical. Moreover, most African countries have joined more than one regional trade organisation. Since their civil services have limited capacity to engage in complex trade negotiations, the result is stalemate: none of the many trade bodies make real progress in pushing ahead with real liberalisation. Instead, commitments to cutting tariff and non-tariff trade barriers rarely move from the treaty-texts to statute books, or from statute to actual implementation.

For the sub-Saharan nations to grow, they must trade more both with the rest of the world, and with each other. However, there is a need for the international community to help move this process forward. It is extremely unlikely that any African government will be willing unilaterally to lower trade barriers, whatever economic theory says about the potential benefits of so doing. Instead, Africa's major trade partners, the EU and the US, will have to open up their economies to trade with African countries.[8] Although the US, through the African Growth and Opportunity Act (AGOA), and the EU through its "Everything but Arms Initiative", claim to offer Africa considerable access to their markets, in practise they offer much less. They must be prepared genuinely to open up their markets, and to explain the limited cost of this to domestic producers. If African exports grew at 10% a year for a decade they would still only account for 5% of total EU imports. The fact that many EU governments opposed parts of the SA-EU free trade deal, almost scuppering it entirely, indicates how dramatically attitudes need to change.

Donors to Africa must also be willing to acknowledge that they are as much a part of the current problem as they are part of the solution. In the past, they have continued to support governments' misguided economic policies, despite their obvious failure. The classic example of this is Tanzania. An internal World Bank study of its own and other donor lending concluded that between 1967 and 1987 donors provided US$15bn of support to what the Bank called a "poorly thought out socialist experiment", even noting that senior WB officials indulged the Tanzanian government without seeking to explain what was realistic and feasible in terms of economic development.[9]

Over the years, donors have simply failed to face up to the reality that many political leaders in sub-Saharan African have becoming experts at playing the "aid game". This is most clearly highlighted in the work of Patrick Chabal and Jean-Pascal Daloz.[10] They argue that African political leaders have agreed to implement donor-inspired reform programmes – in particular IMF and World Bank-sponsored structural adjustment programmes – not because they believed in them, but because "they were the price to pay for continued assistance".

More importantly, although structural adjustment programmes theoretically required strict implementation of reform, notably fiscal consolidation, in practise the international community found itself negotiating an imperfect series of reforms with the flawed leaderships of weak states. Many have never been implemented. For example, a key reform closely identified with structural adjustment programmes is privatisation. Yet, as shown in a recent study for the Economic Commission for Africa, African states have so far only privatised about 40% of their state-owned assets – often the least important ones – despite 20 years of trying.

Donor support is also undermined by "faddism". Privatisation was very much a reform of the 1980s and 1990s, but is now less of priority, even though minimal progress has been made. Having slipped off the policy agenda, it is forgotten. In the area of rural development, the fashionable policies of the 1980s were price liberalisation, and demonopolisation of state-owned crop marketing boards. In the '90s they were replaced by a new agenda of micro-credits, rural safety nets, gender issues and environmental sustainability. Today, the buzzwords are good governance, sector-wide development and poverty eradication.

While these ideas are not wrong in themselves – and may even be important – the problem is that they have taken up the attention of governments who have not even implemented the first wave of reform. Throughout sub-Saharan Africa, crop marketing boards still exist, and agricultural prices are still distorted. Ghanaian cocoa farmers still find it more profitable to smuggle their crop over the border to neighbouring Côte d'Ivoire – because they get a better price there – than to sell through the state cocoa board. Côte d'Ivoire itself, despite attempts at reform, has made only partial progress in developing a more market-oriented system to buy and sell cocoa. Similarly, the Tanzanian government's 2001 *Agricultural Sector Development Strategy* made depressing reading, stating that levels of agricultural growth achieved in the 1990s were too low to pull the majority of the rural poor out of abject poverty. "The root of the problem", the policy document admitted, "has been the poor incentive structure. This has made the sector unprofitable". Although crop boards were identified as a major problem in the country's first structural adjustment programmes in the mid-1980s, and a range of studies have shown them to be bureaucratic, inefficient and corrupt (the word that crops up with monotonous frequency is "parasitic"), nearly 20 years later, they still exist.

While it cannot be denied that the African elite's commitment to economic reform is still relatively weak, there are signs of gradual change. South Africa has an excellent policy regime, which commands the support of most of the country's leading politicians, and which has, in many ways, defined the country's political agenda over the last decade. Tanzanian economic policy formulation has undergone a radical transformation in the last five years, to the point where the Ministry of Finance refuses to loosen its strict cash budgeting system despite the exhortations of donors (although it has relaxed this rigid stance in the last year or so.) Ghana's President Kufuor has campaigned on his determination to improve fiscal discipline, even if he has struggled to achieve it in practice.

While such commitment often seems confined to presidents and some senior ministers – with members of parliament remaining strongly anti-reform – in fact, the shift runs deeper. A visitor to ministries of finance and central banks around the sub-continent finds a cohort of young, but relatively senior, civil servants who are committed to trying to improve economic policy. For them, this commitment is neither rhetorical nor designed to ensure that donors remain on board, but born of the realisation that reform is the only way forward for their countries.

Although it is too early to know for sure, this commitment can also be seen at a political level in the development of the New Economic Partnership for African Development (NEPAD). Theoretically led by three presidents – Olusegun Obasanjo of Nigeria, Abdoulaye Wade of Senegal and Thabo Mbeki of South Africa – NEPAD's real driving force is Mbeki. His vision is that African leaders rather than donors will establish the political reform agenda, and monitor its implementation. While it is easy to dismiss NEPAD as little more than wishful thinking, it is potentially important. Although reform-minded African leaders are unlikely to ever convince their more recalcitrant colleagues to change their ways, reinforcing reform in each other's countries will have a positive impact. Wavering governments might be encouraged to press ahead with difficult changes, rather than letting their reform agenda slide.

NEPAD might also develop an important peacemaking role, as demonstrated by existing attempts to construct African solutions for African problems. The South African government has taken the lead in trying to find political solutions to long-term crises in the Democratic Republic of Congo and Burundi, with some tentative signs of success. (On the other hand, it has made no comparable effort with its northern neighbour, Zimbabwe.) West African leaders have been at the forefront of efforts to try and resolve the political crisis in Côte d'Ivoire. A number of African governments have provided troops to implement the various peace agreements, including South Africa in DRC and Burundi, Nigeria in Liberia, and members of the Economic Community of West Africa in Côte d'Ivoire. There is also a strong likelihood that with the help of EU funding, an African rapid reaction force will be established, for swift deployment in pursuit of limited objectives. Long-term conflict-reduction measures such as these can only be good for sub-Saharan Africa, both in terms of lessening negative publicity and boosting economic development.[11]

There is no magic shortcut to economic development. The simple answer for governments is to get their economic policies right and to boost trade: both with neighbours and with the rest of the world. In the case of sub-Saharan Africa, the vital first step is to achieve macroeconomic stability and to push through agricultural reform. Although Africa is rapidly urbanising – over 50% of the population will soon live in urban areas, according to UN projections – the war on poverty begins in the countryside. Agricultural growth will, in turn, drive urban growth, as well as creating new markets for domestic producers of goods and services.

With these achievements in place, African governments can turn to the task of exploiting niches in global markets. Both the sub-Saharan African states that have a degree of integration with the global economy follow this formula. Mauritius specialises in making knitwear for export, and South Africa does the same with cars and furniture. Other gaps exist for those governments that are willing to interact with the global economy – most obviously, in agricultural processing, basic manufacturing and the provision of services. The development of a horticulture industry in a number of African countries in the 1990s is one of the best examples of this. Should the rich world threaten a protectionist backlash, African governments can point out that even if African exports were to grow at double digits for a decade, they would still only represent a tiny percentage of developed country imports.

All these themes and ideas are clearly illustrated by the case studies in this book. They highlight the fact that, while economic growth is possible in Africa, it is still difficult to know how much it is the result of donor inflows and pressure, and how much to the credit of genuine domestic commitment to change. They also demonstrate that there are limits to sub-Saharan growth without continuing development in the region's five large economies – South Africa, Nigeria, Kenya, Côte d'Ivoire and Zimbabwe. All the sub-Saharan countries need also actively to engage with their neighbours and the global economy. These are the challenges if Asia's tigers are to be chased by African lions.

<hr>

1   'Ripples of a Revolution' by Michael Holman and Michela Wrong, Financial Times, 6th May 1997. However, less than a year later the same authors wrote a second article titled 'Africa's New Leaders Start to Lose Gloss', Financial Times, 23rd March 1998.

2   According to Global Development Finance 2003, published by the World Bank, net resource flow

to sub-Saharan Africa fell from US$26,764m in 1999 to US$18,373m in 2002 (around the same level as in 1990.) 'Net resource flow' includes net long term debt flows, net foreign direct investment and portfolio investment flows and grants (excluding technical co-operation grants).

3   The South African parastatal power utility, Eskom, has quite advanced plans to develop a sub-Saharan African power grid based on the hydro-electric potential of the Democratic Republic of Congo. Southern Africa already has an extensive regional grid, which could easily be connected to Tanzania and the rest of east Africa via Zambia.

4   Although the efforts of the Zimbabwean company, Econet Wireless International, which has operations in Zimbabwe, Botswana, Lesotho, South Africa, Nigeria and Morocco, cannot be ignored.

5   Jeffery Sachs and Andrew Warner, Natural Resource Abundance and Economic Growth, Harvard Institute for International Development (1987).

6   Speaking at a press conference associated with the tenth anniversary of the global anti-corruption organisation, Transparency International, on 7 September 2003, Nigerian president Olusegun Obasanjo declared that his country would be publishing the revenues it receives from its oil industry in line with the principles of the UK government-led Extractive Industries Transparency Initiative. However, he also noted that Nigeria will "tailor the EITI templates to suit the circumstances of its oil and gas sector". He also stated that his government was supportive of the principles of the NGO-led campaign Publish What You Pay – although he noted that confidence would be improved if companies individually published their payments, allowing comparison of the two data sets.

7   This sentiment was perhaps best summed in an article in iafrica.com, whose feature story on the 16th September 2002 was "Trade talk's failure seen as a victory for Africa". However, similar sentiments were expressed in newspapers throughout the continent, and by many African representatives at the talks in Cancun.

8   As argued by Arvind Panagariya ('Think Again: International Trade', in *Foreign Policy* November December 2003), although tariffs in rich countries are highest for labour-intensive products, which is where developing countries have a comparative advantage, in general tariffs for rich nations average 3% on industrial goods compared to 12% in poor countries. Developed countries must also seek to reform their own systems of agricultural subsidy and protection, although the implications of this for many sub-Saharan African countries could be mixed.

9   Another damming case is the ongoing provision of aid to Zaire under President Mboutu, as eloquently highlighted by Michela Wrong in Chapter 9 of *In The Footsteps of Mr Kurtz* , Fourth Estate (2000).

10   A concise and readable summary of these arguments can be found in Patrick Chabal, 'The quest for good governance and development in Africa: is Nepad the answer?' *International Affairs* Vol. 78, No. 3 (2002).

11   Paul Collier of the World Bank and Anke Hoeffler of the Centre for African Studies at Oxford University have recently finished a series of papers on the impact of civil war on African states. They argue that in a typical civil war, incomes are 15% lower than they would have been otherwise. Various papers are available on the websites of both these institutions.

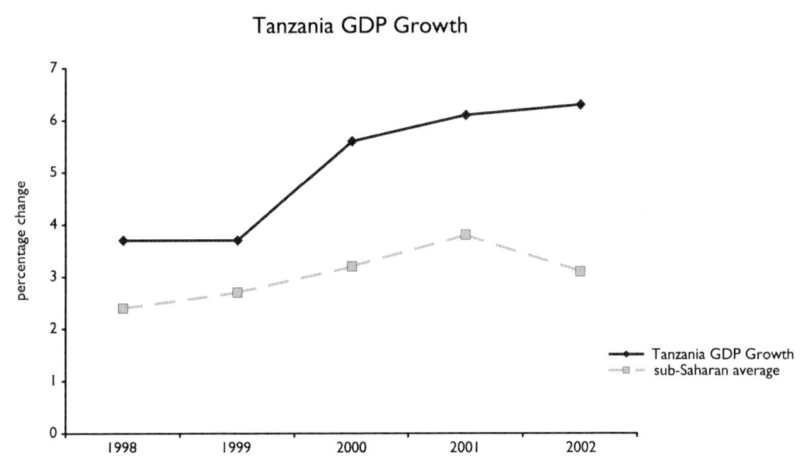

Source: IMF World Economic Outlook, September 2003

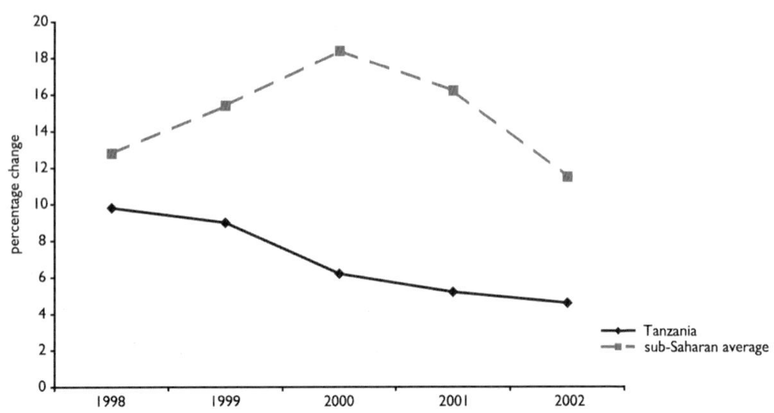

Source: IMF World Economic Outlook, September 2003

1. Tanzania

Brian Cooksey

For Tanzania, macro-economic stabilisation has been the great success of a decade and a half of International Monetary Fund-inspired reforms. Inflation has fallen from 33% in 1985 to around 4.3% currently. The government no longer prints money to finance large budget deficits. Banks no longer extend open-ended credit lines to non-performing public corporations, crop authorities and cooperative unions. Foreign investment has increased steadily, reaching US$224m in 2001. GPD growth has risen from 0.4% in 1994 to 6.3% in 2002, comfortably outstripping population growth of 2.9% a year.

But though stabilisation has boosted headline growth figures, it has done little to raise the living standards of most Tanzanians. Household Budget Surveys suggest that reductions in poverty during the 1990s were insignificant. According to the Government of Tanzania's Poverty and Human Development Report of 2002, the percentage of the population experiencing food poverty (measured against a basket of basic foodstuffs), fell from 21.6% in 1991-92 to 18.7% in 2000-01. 'Basic needs' poverty was not much reduced either, falling from 38.6% to 35.7%. For the same period, the Gini coefficient – a measure of income inequality – rose from 0.34 to 0.37, with income gaps widening most sharply in Dar es Salaam. Urban unemployment also rose during the 1990s, reaching 26% in Dar es Salaam by 2000.

While the figures above may not be very robust, opinion polls also paint a gloomy picture of deepening poverty and growing social inequality. A survey of three thousand households in seven regions, by the NGO Research on Poverty Alleviation (REPOA), in October 2003 found that 90% of respondents believe that only a minority of Tanzanians have benefited from reform, and that for the rest, things are as bad as they were before or worse. Similarly, an Afrobarometer survey of 2001 found that 60% of respondents agreed with the statement 'The government's economic policies have hurt most people and only benefited a few.' Large majorities thought public policy performance failed in creating jobs and food security, or in reducing poverty and the rich-poor gap. In another recent national survey, REPOA found nearly two-thirds of respondents agreeing that 'The gap between rich and poor people has worsened over the last five years'.

Cut the crop boards

Observers offer competing explanations as to why structural adjustment has failed significantly to dent the grinding poverty experienced by the average Tanzanian. Some blame the reforms, others the *non-implementation* of the reforms. To try to understand what is happening, let us first look at the rural economy.

Most poor Tanzanians live in rural areas. Accordingly, investment in agriculture is seen, both by government and by donors, as key to poverty reduction. Prior to the early 1990s, government-owned crop boards and cooperative unions provided credit for inputs such as seeds, fertilizer and pesticides, and were in turn the sole marketing outlet for Tanzania's traditional export crops – coffee, cotton, cashew, tea, tobacco, sisal and pyrethrum. Maize and other grain marketing was the monopoly of the National Milling Corporation. Under pressure from donors, this system was gradually dismantled through the late 1980s and 1990s, bringing in competition between cooperatives and private traders, and leaving export crop boards responsible for issuing trading licences and assuring competition and quality control.

However, current policy and legislation seem designed to 'bring the state back in'. Laws regulating coffee, tobacco and sugar markets were passed in 2001. Crop boards were given powers to be both players in as well as regulators of their respective markets. For example, the Coffee Board 'may perform any commercial activity or hold interest in any undertaking, enterprise or project associated with the coffee industry.' Fines and possible prison sentences await farmers who plant unauthorised seeds. Under the new laws, the Minister of Agriculture appoints the majority of board members. If he is not happy with a board's performance he is empowered to bypass it altogether.

The unambiguous statist thrust of the new Acts reflects a consensus amongst the Tanzanian political class that market liberal-isation is no longer a viable policy option. 'We tried liberalisation, but it didn't work, so we're going back to the old system' seems to be the sentiment. Structural adjustment, it is argued, dealt a body blow to farmers by making inputs such as fertilizer prohibitively expensive, and farm-gate prices low and volatile.

This argument implies that in the pre-adjustment period farmers were relatively prosperous and secure. Indeed, senior politicians and academic researchers frequently argue this case. Unfortunately, it is nonsense. For example, World Bank economist Benno Ndulu points out that in 1980 Kenyan coffee farmers received 98% of the international coffee price, while Tanzanians only got 37%. A Dutch-financed survey of 1984 found that most farming households lacked even basic necessities such as salt, sugar, soap, kerosene and clothing. Claims that the government's agricultural research and advisory services have collapsed due to IMF-inspired budget cuts also miss the main point: with notable exceptions, these services were mediocre at the best of times.

Research seems to show that many farmers also think in terms of the 'good old (pre-reform) days'. This, at least, is what emerges from 'participatory poverty assessments' and 'focus groups', in which farmers often complain they no longer have access to subsidised fertiliser or a guaranteed market for their crops. But broader, quantative surveys come up with quite different findings. For example, the REPOA survey cited above found that two-thirds of rural household heads preferred wholly private or mixed cooperative/private marketing system, and only a quarter wanted to return to a cooperative monopoly. A 1997 survey by TADREG found a majority of farmers in favour of private rather than state-controlled markets. Why do survey and qualitative results contradict each other? Probably because focus-group participants are recruited from among the better-off farmers who may indeed have benefited from the old system, rather than the silent majority who did not. Widely-shared prejudices against 'greedy' Asian traders, foreign – particularly South African – investors and globalisation in general, also influence public perceptions and assessments of liberalisation.

Further evidence that genuine liberalisation of agricultural markets does help farmers comes from Tanzania's landlocked neighbour Uganda. During the 1990s, Uganda downgraded the Ministry of Agriculture, with the result that coffee exports rose dramatically and rural poverty fell year on year, albeit not for the very poorest. By the end of the decade Uganda was earning more from coffee exports than Tanzania earned from all agricultural exports combined. In 2000, when private buyers in Tanzania's north-western region of Kagera had their trading licences summarily revoked, farmers began smuggling coffee to Uganda rather than selling it for a pittance to cooperative unions. This comparison also demonstrates that the benefits from export trade liberalisation should be immediate – there is no need to wait for a 'trickle-down' effect to kick in.

Private investment in agriculture is as critical as government investment, yet donors as well as government seem fixated with state-sponsored investments. The US$57m World Bank-financed 'Participatory Agricultural Development and Empowerment Project', for example, relies on district councils for its implementation. However – as proven by consistent failure in the past – government's ability to function as a routine service deliverer is highly constrained by inadequately trained technical staff, lack of motivation, supervision and discipline, corruption, and a 'sticks' rather than 'carrots' disposition on the part of government officials. Despite the rhetoric of participation and empowerment, project loans from the World Bank and other donor agencies play into the hands of the bureaucracy and the political class, fuelling the politics of patronage. At the same time, increasing ministry budgets – as currently fashionable 'basket finance' does – is unlikely to provide any additional benefits to farmers: most of the increased budget is absorbed by the national and local bureaucracy leaving little or nothing to 'deliver' to farmers.

I do not mean to suggest that 'free' – unregulated – markets are the obvious and only solution to the institutional problems faced by Tanzanian farmers. Markets fail for many reasons, and I have only mentioned a few. But I do suggest that the state's weaknesses as a service provider, and the conflation of regulatory and commercial roles on the part of the crop boards, constitute serious blockages to the emergence of a dynamic rural economy. I am also convinced that aid actually undermines the emergence of a viable agricultural and rural development policy, by empowering central and local government officials who cannot be held accountable for their deeds and misdeeds, further distorting markets and discouraging private investment and enterprise.

Doing a de Soto

Land ownership and use are crucial components of the debate on market liberalisation and poverty reduction. Those favouring foreign investment in agriculture and ranching are pushing for investors' right to buy rather than simply lease land, a right that the 1999 National and Village Land Acts specifically denies. Those concerned for community and smallholder rights, and rights to seasonal pasture for pastoralists, argue that the 1999 legislation is inadequate, being, according to political scientist Sholto Cross, 'predicated on elaborate procedures for certification, whose bureaucratic requirements may well tilt the actual practices of land access in favour of a literate elite.' They also fear that privatisation would lead to an influx of commercial farmers from Southern Africa.

The 'pro-investor' lobby wants to revise the land acts to allow for 'radical title', so that property can be used as security for bank loans. A way around the issue has been proposed through a 'Land Bank', whereby investors would acquire land directly from the Tanzania Investment Centre, which claims to have already identified 'surplus' land for the purpose. The Ministry of Agriculture is also actively looking for investors in huge state-owned estates and ranches, for which the current National Land Act tenurial restrictions constitute a stumbling block.

These legal and policy issues have not prevented the development of a flourishing market in land, and growing differentiation among farmers. Tanzania's ruling class owns large amounts of land, but generally fail to develop it for commercial purposes. Policy-makers aspire to promote the emergence of a class of larger, prosperous 'yeoman' farmers, but have not yet faced up to the fact that this would also entail the emergence of a class of landless wage-labourers. Talk of poverty reduction policies that protect the land rights of the poorest of the poor simply ignores the realities of capitalist development. By the same token, a successful agricultural policy reduces dramatically the number of people employed in the mindless drudgery of agricultural life, and increases the number in industry and services. Even where poverty is widespread, there are farmers with much more land and livestock than others, and a wider range of non-agricultural income-generating opportunities.

New and well maintained roads – a core policy priority – increase land prices, and the rich begin to buy out the poor. Drought has the same effect among cattle owners. (Tanzania is in its second year of serious drought, and is receiving food aid). As a result of the above trends, the rural landless population is already growing in number. The problem is, there are too few opportunities for gainful employment outside agriculture: there is no discernable upward spiral of development. Many poor young men go into artisanal mining, others seek 'informal sector' employment in town.

New investment in mining and tourism has boosted Tanzania's growth rate in recent years. Mineral exports (mostly gold) were worth US$431m in 2003, more than twice the value of Tanzania's six main agricultural exports combined. Modern mining generates natural resource rents that increase government revenues and foreign exchange earnings, but is not 'pro-poor' in the direct sense of creating significant employment opportunities. Indeed, small-scale, labour-intensive artisanal mining – which is said to employ anything up to a million people, producing an estimated 17 tonnes of gold in 2001 – is seriously threatened by the foreign investment that has poured into the sector in recent years. Other relevant issues are the leniency of the investment agreements (too soft on the mining companies?) and the degree of illicit plundering going on (smuggling, theft). Despite receiving a US$10m World Bank loan to speed up and clarify licencing procedures, mining sector regulation remains poor. The risks, particularly for small and medium investors, who are essential for a balanced mineral sector development, are considerable.

The good news is that, to date, disputes over Tanzania's natural resources have not led to the systematic corruption, plunder, violence and social disruption that is common in other countries, the Democratic Republic of Congo being the nearest example. The

Pants to property rights

World-famous Peruvian economist and ideologue Hernando de Soto was in Dar es Salaam recently, expounding his thesis on why capitalism is successful in some countries and not in others. He argues that most private property in poor countries – particularly land and housing – is 'dead', in that it is not used as a means of investment and accumulation. Property rights are poorly developed and entering the 'formal' capitalist economy presents formidable time – and money-consuming bureaucratic obstacles, as de Soto long ago demonstrated in the slums of Lima. (Obtaining a license for a small business, he discovered, took 289 days and cost 31 times the average monthly minimum wage). Tanzania's ruling class listened carefully as de Soto, who with President Benjamin Mkapa chairs the World Commission on the Social Dimension of Globalisation, spelled out the solution to capitalism's Third World failure: develop property rights for the poor. One senior government official pointed out privately after the presentation that the politicians and private businessmen who routinely fail to pay back the large loans they obtain from banks and other government and parastatal institutions would risk losing the property they put up as collateral *if* property rights were effectively formalised and legally binding. Lesson: formalising the property of the rich is also a major challenge.

The week after de Soto's visit I observed Dar es Salaam City Council militiamen and women summarily destroying the temporary stands of fast food vendors and retailers in various parts of the city centre. The next day the government issued a ban on imported second-hand underwear, sold mostly through informal sector outlets. An official of the Tanzania Bureau of Standards told the BBC World Service that second-hand underwear poses a health hazard, that local manufacturers can produce the imported items, and that it is somehow unseemly for Tanzanian women to buy the 'rich world's' cast-off bras and panties. Research suggests that the minimalist thongs favoured by Dar es Salaam's middle and working class girls are not manufactured locally.

Tanzanian government has, however, used mining to finance military procurement outside the budget. Merimeta, a joint venture between the Ministry of Defence and South African investors, was set up for this purpose, but collapsed leaving the Ministry US$130m in debt. How much Merimeta in fact realised from gold sales, and what happened to the money, is still unclear.

In summary, if stabilisation is to produce sustained, poverty-reducing economic growth, there will have to be a lot more saving and investment in agriculture and agro-processing, industry and the service sector. This will require a transformation in the current approach to taxation and regulation, and the creation of institutions that promote rather than frustrate overall rural development. There is little sign that this is happening. The reason why most people feel worse off and perceive inequality to be rising is – arguably – because they are experiencing these phenomena at first hand.

Private and informal

Although the relative size of the informal economy is difficult to estimate, 'informalisation' is widely considered to be one of the main consequences of structural adjustment. Whilst black markets in most consumer goods and foreign exchange are things of the past, there is little doubt that the number and type of informal enterprises has mushroomed under market liberalisation. The closure of many state enterprises, preceded or followed by staff cuts, has stimulated the creation of both formal and informal (ie unregistered and untaxed) small-scale enterprises.

Despite their growing numbers, petty producers and traders often struggle to survive, and are usually subjected to official harassment rather than support. Despite the establishment of a National Micro-Finance Bank (NMB), and of various NGOs specialising in small-scale loans, most small enterprises are frustrated in their efforts to grow and formalise through lack of affordable credit, training and tax incentives, or a conducive regulatory environment. The 1995 Dar es Salaam Informal Sector Survey found that 95% of financing for small enterprises still comes from personal resources, family and friends.

In some cases, privatisation has been an unqualified commercial success; breweries, cement works and sugar estates, for example. A number of private management contracts, as opposed to out-and-out privatisation, have also increased the efficiency and profitability of remaining state-owned firms. The Dar es Salaam harbour container-terminal has been successfully taken out of the hands Tanzania Harbours Authority, leading to a dramatic improvement in container turnaround times. Similarly, in the twelve months since Net Solutions was awarded a management contract by the electricity utility Tanesco, it has collected TShs90bn (approx US$90m) of unpaid power bills.

Despite these gains, management contracts are often criticised on the grounds that expatriate managers are paid too much, that their local counterparts are marginalised and exploited, that profit repatriation is excessive (even ideologically unacceptable), that they fail to deliver on contractual agreements, and so on. An alternative, softer option is the Executive Agencies (EA) concept, whereby government departments have to compete with private contractors for contracts. These are now widespread, having been adopted for government services as diverse as statistics-gathering, road maintenance and bore-hole drilling.

However, there are major problems with EAs, as experience in Tanzania and elsewhere demonstrates. Regulating them requires capacity and probity – the widespread absence of which justified setting them up in the first place. When a central government service unit is restructured to compete with private providers for contracts, it is unlikely that competition will be fair. More importantly, EAs are still vulnerable to pressures from the parent ministry. In the recent case of the Tanzania Roads Fund (TANROADS), for example, not only was a substantial number of operational staff transferred from the Ministry of Works to TANROADS, but parallel decision-making structures were created, for example, in tendering. Despite receiving substantial funds from an earmarked fuel tax, Dar es Salaam's heavily used roads are still maintained and repaired in a profoundly casual and perfunctory manner, unless additional aid money is involved. Official regulatory bodies for the various public/private service providers – telecommunications, power supply, water – are similarly vulnerable to manipulation. For example, the recent refusal of the regulator to reduce the (exorbitant) charges for cellular phone calls pending the contracting of an 'international consultancy' on tariffs, suggests manipulation by a well-connected cellphone cartel.

Both privatisation and liberalisation are vulnerable to populist demagoguery, in that often their most visible beneficiaries are often not the *wazawa* – indigenous Tanzanians – but foreigners and the country's Asian and Arab business communities. Former Minister of Trade and Industry Iddi Simba, who at one time attempted to ban foreigners from certain industrial and commercial sectors, is the most notable for this view.

The main beneficiary of nearly two decades of liberalisation are Asian traders and industrialists, an emerging class of African politicians, bureaucrats, businessmen (and women), and actors within 'civil society'. In all these sectors one finds industrious and socially responsible groups and individuals doing good work. Those who have benefited most, however, are the 'straddlers' and the systematically corrupt. 'Straddling' means having a foot (or a hand) in different sectors, or moving rapidly from one to another. Senior civil servants become politicians; politicians join the private sector; their wives run donor-funded NGOs. For businesses, corruption means enrichment through tax evasion and cronyism. For politicians and bureaucrats, it is the other side of this coin, plus the plundering of state coffers and diversion of aid receipts. A range of secondary operators service and sometimes join this class, including academics, consultants, lawyers, accountants and some local aid-workers.

If the above seems an exaggeration, one only has to look at the type of construction going on in Dar es Salaam's 'middle-class' residential suburbs, and count the number of luxury vehicles on the roads, to register the obvious fact of rapid and fabulous enrichment. How much of this is honest returns to honest labour, and how much not, is an issue for further research.

Good and bad governance

For nearly a decade, donors have stressed good governance and commitment to fighting corruption as preconditions for aid. But in practice, the Tanzanian government only risks invoking conditionalities, including aid cuts, in very extreme circumstances. The general rule is that donors are under pressure to move money and to protect (and if possible increase) their budgets, even if it means turning a blind eye to corruption and systematic failure to meet other formal

Independent Power Tanzania Ltd:
Public-Private Partnership at its worst

IPTL is an Independent Power Project (IPP) funded by Malaysian investors Mechmar Bhd. The deal - to supply 100 megawatts of power using diesel generators on a use or pay basis - was hotly contested by donors and consultants on the grounds of cost, choice of technology, and projected demand for power. After much local and international legal wrangling, and accusations of high-level official corruption, the project was finally commissioned in January 2002. During its first year of operation, IPTL cost US$40m in capacity payments alone, and functioned at less than 10% of installed capacity. The Finnish contractor Wärtsilä – which currently operates the IPTL plant under a management contract – is implicated in colluding with the Malaysian investor to inflate the price of the power generators by at least US$10m.

Bilateral donors worry that the US$70m they have granted for general budget support this year is helping finance IPTL through a US$2.5m monthly power subsidy from the Treasury to the Ministry of Energy and Minerals. But although donors have expressed their opposition to IPTL over the years, they are currently avoiding the issue publicly, so as not to upset the post-HIPC honeymoon.

In his 2003/04 budget speech, Minister of Energy and Minerals Daniel Yona admitted that IPTL power was too expensive, and said the government was looking for funds to buy the plant. If it runs for the agreed 20 years, IPTL is potentially ten times more costly than the BAe radar deal (see main text), but has not received one tenth of the international press coverage.

aid conditions. The bigger the aid programme, the more likely denial of corruption and 'slippage' in reform implementation. President Mkapa, who came to power in 1995 pledging to deal with corruption, is widely seen to have lost the fight. The IPTL saga (see Box) is often cited as proof of his reluctance or inability to deal with high-level corruption in party and government.

The kind of good-governance indicators donors prefer concern inputs and processes – for example, anti-corruption laws passed, reports published, budgets funded and staff recruited – rather than concrete outputs – number of officials prosecuted or value of corruptly-acquired assets returned to the state. Were conditionalities tagged to impact, there would be a risk of governments failing to meet them, forcing donors to invoke penalties, or explain why they do not do so. If good performance rather than declarations of intent triggered aid, the same problem would arise. Consequently, conditionalities are almost always 'ex ante' rather than 'ex post.'

As they move away from specific project-funding towards general poverty-reduction budget support, donors are more than ever concerned that their aid should be seen to be properly used. Big bilateral donors such as the UK's Department for International Development (DfID) naturally aspire to aid only those countries that are serious about fighting corruption. In 2001, British Overseas Development Secretary Clare Short crossed swords with the Tanzanian government over the purchase of a US$40m radar system from British Aerospace, a leading arms manufacturer, just after Tanzania obtained pledges of international debt relief under the Heavily Indebted Poor Countries (HIPC) programme. Reports suggested that the radar system was overpriced and inappropriate for Tanzanian needs. Ms Short claimed but did not prove that the deal was corrupt, and British budget support to Tanzania was temporarily halted. Prime minister Tony Blair supported the deal and eventually budget support was restored. Ms Short mended her bridges with President Mkapa, and Britain subsequently increased its aid commitments to Tanzania by 50%.

Aiders and abetters

Official aid to Tanzania finances most of its development budget and about a third of recurrent expenditure. Total aid flows rose from US$2.3bn during the 1970s to US$7bn during the 1980s and US$7.8 for 1990-97. They now average US$1bn a year. Aid finances balance of payments support, debt relief, direct budget support, basket funding and project financing. Of these, the latter is declining while basket funding and direct budget support are rising, but detailed analysis is difficult since a significant proportion of donor spending is still not captured in government budgets.

The perils of aid are well-known: it crowds out investment, substitutes for local taxation, provides perverse incentives *not* to reform, undermines local accountability, carries heavy transaction costs for recipients, distorts public sector incentive structures and creates foreign debt. All these weaknesses are demonstrable in the Tanzanian case (most strikingly, the tax take is an extraordinarily low 12-13% of GNP).

Though some of these problems – for example, debt and high transaction costs – are fixable, others are inherent. It follows that the volume of aid to a particular country must obey the law of diminishing marginal returns, with negative returns after a certain point. Yet the debate on foreign aid in the developed world assumes a highly elastic 'absorptive capacity' on the part of recipient countries, with the main policy aim being that aid commitments reach a set proportion of GDP. This fundamental point is routinely ignored in international debates on aid and new aid initiatives of all kinds.

I would add a more contested inherent weakness of aid to the above daunting list: that aid stimulates corrupt practices. Years of investigating corruption and aid lead me to conclude that aid agencies and their staff are sometimes corrupt; even when they not – and generally they are not – they often encourage waste and corruption among recipients, through disbursement pressures and the tendency to over-fund particular sectors or activities; and there are pressures on donor agencies to hide or ignore the bad news (ineffective projects, suspicion or proof of corruption), reinforcing pressures on government to do the same. My efforts to report examples of grand corruption involving aid have made me more enemies than friends among both aid donors and recipients. I conclude that aid agencies routinely fail to practice the transparency and accountability they require of their development partners.

When analysts claim that aid has had 'no impact' they are missing the point. Rather, the question should be, if aid has not had the *desired* impact, what impact *has* it had? Answers to this question may be sought in psychology (the aid-dependent mentality), social science (aid creates/strengthens patronage networks), and economics. My position – that aid effectiveness is undermined by the practice of various forms of political patronage – prompts one to ask how aid influences the political system in its turn. Neither donors nor aid recipients are very keen to explore these intellectual avenues.

With the rise of budget support, the Tanzanian government and donor agencies have put a lot of effort into improving the efficiency of the budgetary process, in order to refocus spending towards the main 'pro-poor' sectors, especially basic education and healthcare.

Show Me the Money

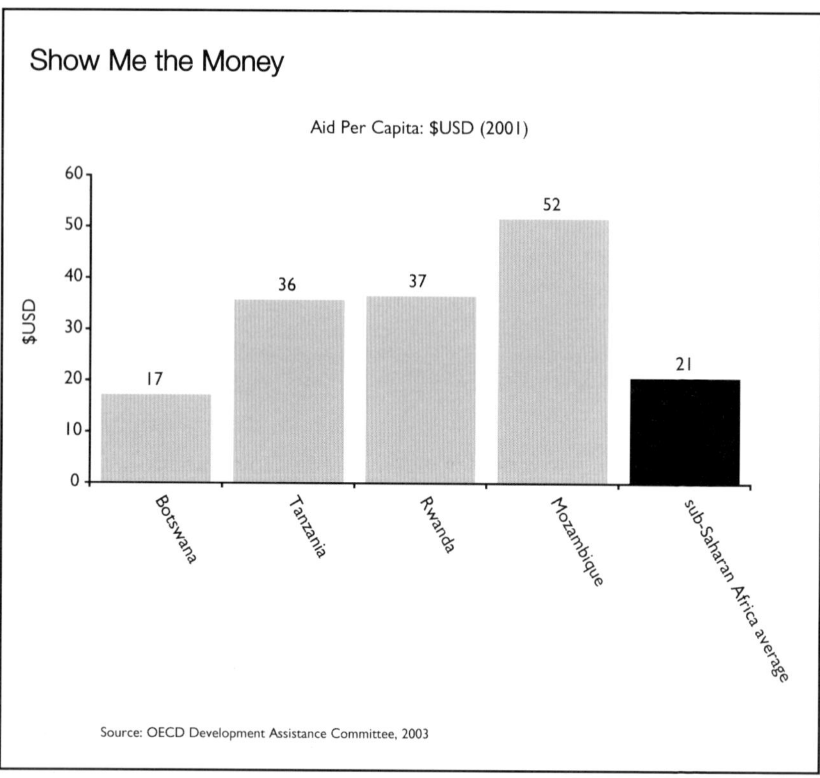

Source: OECD Development Assistance Committee, 2003

Yet there is worrying evidence that, although 'pro-poor' spending has increased significantly under the PRS, 'non-pro-poor' spending has increased just as much. This at least was the tentative conclusion of the External Review of the 2003 Public Expenditure Review by the Danish aid agency Danida and the World Bank.

Non-government organisations claim the government is pursuing contradictory policies in health and education. Whereas primary school fees were abolished in 2000 in a successful bid to increase enrolments, the government plans to extend 'cost-sharing' in the health sector down to the dispensary level. World-Bank inspired

Community Health Funds have been introduced haphazardly across the country despite evidence that the poor simply cannot afford to participate in such schemes. REPOA's Policy and Service Satisfaction Survey cited above found that four out of ten respondents claimed to know of people who had been refused health care through inability to pay consultancy fees, the cost of treatment or unofficial payments to health workers. The cost of healthcare was described as a 'major problem' by over half those interviewed, making health the third most pressing problem facing households (the cost of food and other basic essentials ranked first and second).

Budgeted money often does not reach its intended beneficiaries. An expenditure tracking study undertaken by REPOA and the Economic and Social Research Foundation (ESRF) found that *more than half* of all non-salary expenditure in the health sector did not reach its intended facilities. The annual report of the Controller and Auditor General (CAG) also documents unauthorised and improper expenditure on a huge scale. Rarely do these reports lead to the return of monies misused or the disciplining of officials responsible. The policy of local government decentralisation, designed to 'bring government closer to the people', is widely perceived to have brought corruption closer to the people.

Conclusions

Aid agencies are always looking for a star performer, and for the moment Tanzania is one. But its star status will fade unless the government can come up with *and implement* policies that boost the incomes of the majority poor. For the moment, there is no evidence to suggest that the government has the vision, the will or the capacity to ask the fundamental questions that might allow such a policy to evolve. Although the international financial institutions have helped Tanzania out of the depths of economic collapse brought about by the Nyerere regime, and currently provide most of the foreign exchange to bolster the exchange rate and fill the trade gap, overall the liberalisation policies advocated have not addressed the underlying causes of market failure, and have arguably contributed to that failure.

A number of informed observers believe the move from project to budgetary support under the Poverty Reduction Strategy is a very risky venture, with only a limited shelf-life. They think the state machinery, both national and local, is too vulnerable to corruption and patronage, and bureaucratic sloth and inefficiency, to handle large additional resource flows effectively. We will soon know whether they are right or wrong.

Development agencies such as DfID spend much time and effort thinking about these issues. Yet in their concern to see the Poverty Reduction Strategy work, they are still failing to ask some vital questions. Much is known about the issues that I have raised above, and other important issues – including gender, political pluralism, culture, and HIV/AIDS – that I have left out. Here are some of the questions I think we should now begin to address more systematically. Are political systems based on patronage capable of initiating market reforms that will bring about broad-based growth? What does aid really contribute in such contexts? Is corruption the price we have to pay for political stability, and is it a precondition for the emergence of an African capitalist class that will know why markets matter and do more to make them work? If there are winners and losers from liberalisation, how many are there of each?

The central pillars of neo-liberalism – market liberalisation, privatisation, budgetary austerity – are only useful if they translate into equitable and sustained economic growth. How each of these policies, and other aspects of liberalisation, are managed in practice determines overall growth and poverty outcomes. In all this the state has a major role to play, but not the current role. Those in government who want to roll back these policies, are obliged to tell us how they propose to deal with the problems that led to the need for the reforms in the first place.

Tanzania's most precious assets are sustained peace and political stability. If the government fails to deliver on poverty reduction, they could be threatened. In Tanzania as elsewhere, a growing mass of relatively and absolutely deprived urban youth are fertile ground for religious, nationalist and racist demagogy. I asked at the outset whether poverty reduction can succeed, where structural adjustment failed, in producing a virtuous upward spiral of growth, widely-spread benefits, and improved government services. My answer, unfortunately, is 'no' – not unless we begin to think more deeply about the underlying issues and face up to some unpleasant truths.

Bibliographic note

The *LADDER* research programme on rural livelihoods coordinated by Professor Frank Ellis of the University of East Anglia referred to above can be accessed via <www.odg.uea.ac.uk/ladder>. My work on market liberalisation is part of a research programme known as the *Tanzania Agriculture Situation Analysis* (TASA) undertaken by the Tanzania Development Research Group and financed by the Rockefeller Foundation, DfID, SIDA, and Concern Worldwide. The *Policy and Service Satisfaction Survey* by Research on Poverty Alleviation <repoa@repoa.or.tz> will be published soon. Other references are: Benno Ndulu and Francis Mwega, 'Economic Adjustment Policies', in Joel Barkan (ed) *Beyond Capitalism vs Socialism in Kenya and Tanzania*, East African Publishers Ltd and Lynne Rienner, Nairobi and Boulder, 1994; Hernando de Soto, *The Mystery of Capital: Why Capitalism Triumphs in the West and Fails Everywhere Else*, New York: Basic Books, 2000

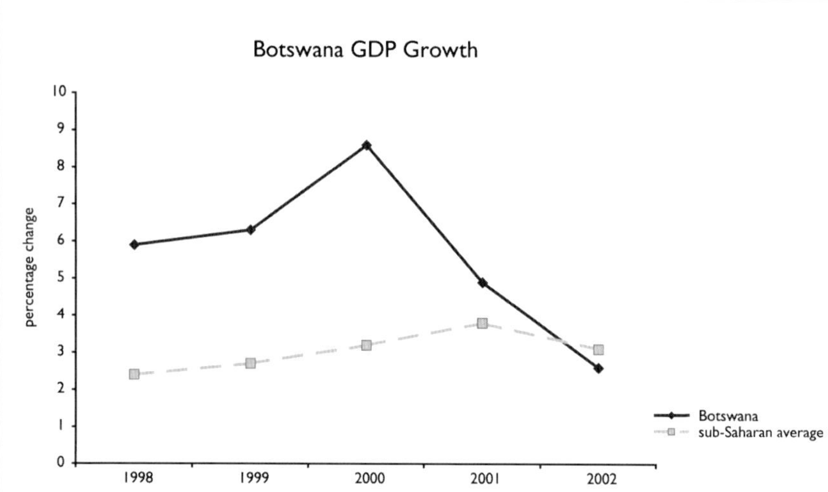

Source: IMF World Economic Outlook, September 2003

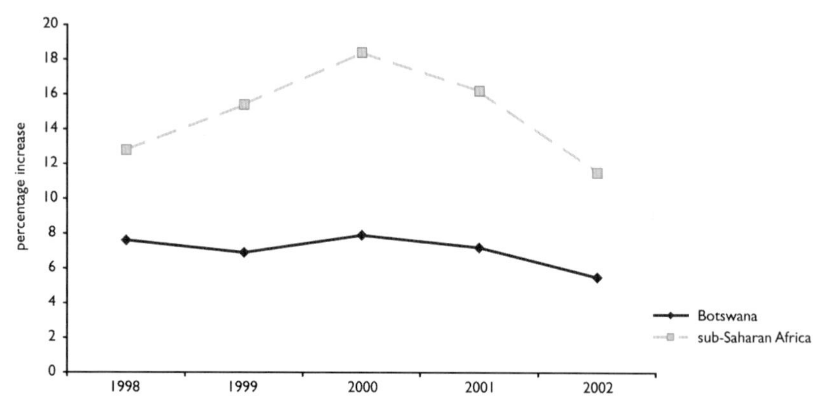

Source: IMF World Economic Outlook, September 2003

2. Botswana

Ian Taylor

The Republic of Botswana is one of Africa's relative success stories. It has been a multi-party democracy (albeit under one party's rule), since independence in 1966, and is perceived as an oasis of stability in a continent wracked by conflict. Its economic growth has been phenomenal: whilst between 1982 and 1991 Africa's annual average growth was around 2%, Botswana's was nearly 11%. Over the last ten years this has settled – barring a dip last year due to lower diamond prices and unrest in Zimbabwe – to annual growth of 5-9%. From being one of the poorest countries in the world at independence, it is now classified by the World Bank as a middle-income country, with GDP per head of $9,500 in 2002. (At independence this stood at the equivalent of US$80 in today's prices.) Its credit ratings are on par with some of the best-performing emerging economies: Moody's recently awarded it an A-plus rating, the highest on the continent.

Nor is Botswana dependent on overseas aid. It is one of only two African states that are net creditors to the IMF and World Bank rather than borrowers, and Overseas Development Assistance (ODA) received as a percentage of GDP is a mere 0.6% – a tiny amount compared to the rest of Africa, where the sub-Saharan average is 11.4%. Through the 1990s the budget remained healthily in surplus, and public debt was insignificant. Today, it is only around 8% of GDP, and Botswana's foreign exchange reserves are about US$6 billion. A projected budget deficit of 1.9 billion pula ($396m), or 3% of GDP, in 2003/4 is blamed on increased government expenditure on AIDS and a dip in mineral revenues.

Thanks to its economic success, Botswana enjoys comprehensive and expanding public services and infrastructure, including 18,300 kilometres of roads (it had 13 kilometres at independence). The road network links all settlements with a population of over 100 people, covering over 90% of the population. Educational and health services, largely absent at independence, have all been developed. The combined enrolment ratio at first, second and third education levels is around 70%, compared with a sub-Saharan average of 44%. This has resulted in a literacy rate of 74%, contrasting with 58% for the rest of the continent. Ninety percent of Botswana's children are enrolled in primary school, and primary health care is available to the 80% of the rural population living within 15 kilometres of a health clinic.

I don't mean rhinestones

Botswana's growth record, and a large chunk of its economy, is based on diamonds. First discovered at Orapa four years after independence, their production has risen to 28m tonnes in 2002. This makes Botswana the world's biggest producer of gem-quality diamonds in terms of value, and the second biggest in terms of volume (Australia is first). However, abundant mineral wealth alone does not explain Botswana's success: as the case of Sierra Leone demonstrates, natural resources can, perversely, sabotage nation-building and development. The additional factors responsible for Botswana's relative success are the focus of this paper.

By the early 1980s, diamonds had replaced beef as Botswana's leading foreign-exchange earner. In 1981, they accounted for 40% of total exports; in 1999 for 74%, and by 2002 they made up 77% of exports and 45% of GDP.

Despite this dependence, Botswana has avoided the economic and political distortions often attendant on the discovery of substantial natural resources. It has achieved this by spending its diamond revenues sensibly, pursuing sound macroeconomic policies, and providing incentives to private investment – all supported by its reputation for political stability. During periods of high diamond prices and production it has not spent all of its revenues, and in leaner times it has refrained from heavy borrowing. There has been a conscious policy to build up foreign exchange reserves: in per capita terms these are now some of the world's largest, sufficient to pay for 26 months' imports. The country has also maintained a liberal exchange-control regime, ensuring that the currency is not over-valued. Finally, development projects are properly budgeted, so that future recurrent spending is accounted for within each project's costs.

Since 1975, ownership of Botswana's diamond mines has been split 50:50 with the diamond cartel De Beers (previously, the split was 85:15

in De Beers' favour.) Negotiated amicably, this arrangement has allowed Botswana to benefit from De Beers' technical and marketing expertise, while retaining influence over wage policies and production levels. Though Botswana has not succeeded in creating a domestic diamond-cutting industry, production costs have been kept low, preserving high mark-ups on the export of uncut stones.

'Development through Unity'

Botswana's emphasis on development spending dates back to the immediate post-independence period. Within the Ministry of Finance, two factions fought over the new country's economic policy. In one corner, Permanent Secretary Alfred Beeby insisted on the need to "balance the books", and refused to consider heavy government spending until finances were available. In the other, a group of young expatriate economists, led by Pierre Landell-Mills and Quill Hermans, favoured pro-active development planning, and aggressive international lobbying for aid and loans.

The latter faction had the ear of Quett Masire, then vice-president. Beeby nonetheless succeeded in having Landell-Mills thrown out of the civil service for "insubordination", briefly causing a rift between Masire and President Khama. A commission of enquiry finally resolved the matter, resulting in the creation of a Ministry of Development Planning (MDP), with Hermans as permanent secretary and Landell-Mills as senior government economist.

It is not an exaggeration to say that the foundations of the Botswanan state were laid during the "Landell-Mills affair", in the sense that ever since, economic policy has been development-driven. In 1970 the MDP became the Ministry of Finance and Development

Planning (MFDP), making explicit the centrality of development to economic management in general. Especially in the early days of independence, it played an extremely important role, identifying development projects via detailed planning, and successfully soliciting funds for them from abroad, at a time when local capital was scarce. Dominating the line ministries dealing with health, education, agriculture and so on, the MFDP boasted a highly professional staff, and even challenged the Office of the President as the premier ministry in Gaborone. Both Khama's successors, Masire and the current president Festus Mogae, served as Minister of Finance and Development Planning before taking office.

With the discovery of diamonds in 1970 the MFDP started to borrow, in the knowledge that loans could be paid off. In 1974 it launched an Accelerated Rural Development Programme, under which were constructed hundreds of new roads, schools, clinics, dams and boreholes. The programme ran alongside other initiatives such as the re-negotiation of the Southern African Customs Union Agreement, under which Botswana won a larger share of customs revenues. These new sources of income enabled Botswana to end its dependence on British grants-in-aid as early as 1972/73, now referred to as the "Year of Our Second Independence". By 1980, diamond receipts allowed Gaborone to pay off all its debts, and the MFDP returned to its former position of not incurring debts in excess of projected state earnings, a policy it largely adheres to today.

A pinch of planning

Though Botswana operates according to national development plans, these envision the state as a facilitator of economic growth and development, rather than a participant. The plans have always taken a market economy context as a given, and made thriving private enterprise a central goal. Similarly, the government spends a relatively modest 40% or so of GDP (Britain's figure for 2001-'02 was 37.1%). Mining is state-controlled in partnership with De Beers (through the Debswana mining company), and cattle-farming is subsidised via a state-purchasing scheme under which exporters take advantage of preferential trade terms with the EU. On the other hand the growing tourism, financial services, construction and manufacturing sectors are in private hands, and relatively unhampered by red tape or competition from state-run rivals. Property and contractual rights, in contrast to many other African states, are generally upheld in the courts. Botswana ranks 54th on the World Economic Forum's Business Competitiveness Index, putting it above all the sub-Saharan countries except for South Africa.

The government has been notably successful in utilising diamond receipts to act as an "entrepreneurial agent". Institutions have been built to stimulate the private sector – the prime example being the Botswana Development Corporation (BDC). Established in 1970 and wholly-owned by the state, the BDC provides loans and equity capital to new private-sector projects that it deems commercially viable, especially those generating sustainable employment. It also builds factory units and shop premises for lease to small enterprises. The Botswana Export Development and Investment Authority (BEDIA), set up in 1997, promotes foreign investment into Botswana, with special emphasis on export-oriented manufacture, and helps domestic exporters penetrate new markets. Despite Hyundai's disappointing closure of a new plant in the mid-90s, BEDIA has been successful in attracting investment from South

Africa, notably into modern shopping malls. Reflecting the close links between the public and private sector, BEDIA's board of directors includes private sector representatives as well as officials from the MFDP and Ministry of Commerce and Industry.

It's the politics, stupid

Obviously, economic policy does not spring from nowhere. In large part, Botswana's development strategy is accounted for by the powerful sway of rural exporters strategically situated at the highest levels of the state and bureaucracy. It is thanks to these close links between government and countryside that Botswana has avoided the widespread "African bias" against rural businesses in favour of the urban areas.

At independence, in contrast to many other parts of Africa, power went to the traditional rural-linked ruling class, rather than to an emergent left-wing intelligentsia. Botswana's first president, Seretse Khama, was typical of post-independence leaders in having been educated in England – he read law at Oxford – but atypical in also being head of the country's dominant tribe, the Bangwato. From annexation (at the request of tribal leaders threatened by encroaching Boers), in 1885, Britain had governed its obscure backwater protectorate, then known as Bechuanaland, with a light hand. Thanks also to the absence of significant white settlement or economic development (diamonds were only discovered after independence), traditional social structures remained largely intact. To this day, one of the main factors accounting for Botswana's relative success is the social chemistry of its different elites – a close web of family and social relationships linking cattle-ranchers, politicians and bureaucrats.

Khama's traditional authority, combined with his personal charisma and adept sidelining of lesser tribal chiefs (see below), meant there was no real opposition to his agenda in the immediate post-independence years. Having been soundly beaten in elections in 1965, embryonic pan-African and socialist parties based in the railway towns failed to challenge him. Instead, during Khama's tenure at least, voters remained steeped in a traditionalist culture of respect for authority, hindering any renegotiation of the post-colonial dispensation or political debate based on class. This gave space for Khama's Botswana Democratic Party (BDP) to establish a hegemonic position, which it has maintained ever since. Opposition parties, though allowed to exist (Botswana has no political prisoners), are disadvantaged by a first-past-the-post electoral system and interminable faction-fighting.

Botswana's post-independence elite was also unusual in preferring private to state-owned economic activity. On independence, the country's only significant assets were its cattle herds, and Khama and his colleagues, being large cattle-owners themselves, were naturally unwilling to see them nationalised or threatened. Consequently, the national leadership – in contrast to virtually everywhere else in Africa – did not come to see the state as a source of self-enrichment, but as a force to be kept within bounds and to promote development.

Typical of Khama's subtle, gradualist approach to state-building was his handling of traditional chiefs. The Chieftainship Act of 1965 gave the president power to recognise, or not recognise, traditional rulers, making all chiefs subordinate to central government. A House of Chiefs was established, but with no legislative powers. Essentially, the new state established new bodies (parliament, land boards, town and district councils, village development committees etc.), that replaced the traditional leaders and transferred authority from the traditional to the modern state. Though the chiefs automatically became *ex-officio* members of local institutions, their positions were dependent on recognition by the state – something that could be (and sometimes was) withdrawn.

Whilst traditional elites were thus incorporated into state structures in independent Botswana, the potency of their newfound roles was profoundly circumscribed. At one blow, potential opponents to the new government were conciliated and defused. Instead, traditional rulers served as facilitators for the implementation of government policy, particularly in the rural areas. Whilst accorded respect and status, their role within Botswana was re-invented so that they became grass-roots agents of government, communicating government programmes at the *kgotla* (village assembly) level. Today, chiefs continue to act as inter-preters of what is going on in Botswana, and contribute to government policy by communicating it to their tribesmen.

Central to the avoidance of inter-ethnic rivalry was the central government's acquisition of mineral rights. Crucially, Khama persuaded his Bangwato tribe to relinquish their communal rights over the newly-discovered diamond and copper/nickel reserves in the former Bangwato Reserve, (now the "Central District".) Once the Bangwato agreed, other tribes followed suit. Mining revenues thus went to the national treasury, rather than to local assemblies or chiefs, and were seen to benefit society as a whole rather than particular ethnic groups.

At your service

Botswana is fortunate in the quality of its civil service. Unusually for Africa, acting civil servants are disqualified by law from standing for public office. This has insulated bureaucrats from party politics, and reinforced the demarcation between government and state.

By African standards, Botswana's civil servants are also well paid, which together with Khama's legacy of clean government and intolerance of graft accounts for the country's relative freedom from corruption. The corruption-watchdog NGO Transparency International rates it the 30th "cleanest" country in the world, tied with Taiwan and above Italy as well as all other African states. Though senior politicians were caught siphoning funds from the Housing Corporation and Development Bank in the early 1990s, there have been no big corruption scandals since, and a powerful, high-profile Directorate on Corruption and Economic Crime encourages whistle-blowing.

The government has made good use of foreign expertise, particularly in preparing national development plans and budgets. In contrast to much of the rest of Africa, many British colonial officials were retained post-independence to help train up a local civil service, allowing a new generation of technocrats smoothly and gradually to take over the running of the country. Other foreign advisors were brought in in the early days of independence to help in institution and capacity-building. The government is still happy to fill posts from overseas where necessary: the current deputy-governor of the national bank is an expatriate and the presidential spokesman American (though now a citizen of Botswana).

The manner by which national development plans are drawn up and, once agreed, are extremely hard to change, prevents the sort of plundering of state funds for political ends common elsewhere. Diamond and taxation revenues transfer out of a Consolidated Fund into three special funds, namely the Domestic Development Fund, which contributes to capital projects; the Revenue Stabilisation Fund, which absorbs short term revenue increases and provides short-term funding to parastatals and local government; and the Public Debt Service Fund, which provides long-term funding to parastatals.

In short, Botswana's civil service is largely honest and effective, and has avoided over-expenditure and other pitfalls associated with developing-world bureaucracies, particularly African ones. It has a demonstrable capacity to take pre-emptive policy action and pursue the long-term interests of the country. Willingness to recruit and retain expatriates as well as well-educated Batswana, combined with a low tolerance for corruption, make it a tool for rather than an obstacle to development. In coalition with the ruling BDP it has succeeded in establishing a solvent state able to deliver public goods (roads, schools, watering facilities, clinics etc) on a non-tribal, non-regional basis.

AIDS and inequality

Botswana is not, of course, a utopia in the Kalahari. The country faces serious problems related to equity and life chances – most dramatically, HIV/AIDS. Its infection rate of 39% is one of the world's highest, meaning that of its total population of 1.7m, a staggering 330,000 currently carry an incurable fatal disease. As many babies are infected in four days, as are in a whole year in the United States, and average life expectancy has just dipped below forty, for the first time in half a century. By 2010, according to the health studies department of the American census bureau, it will have fallen to 27.

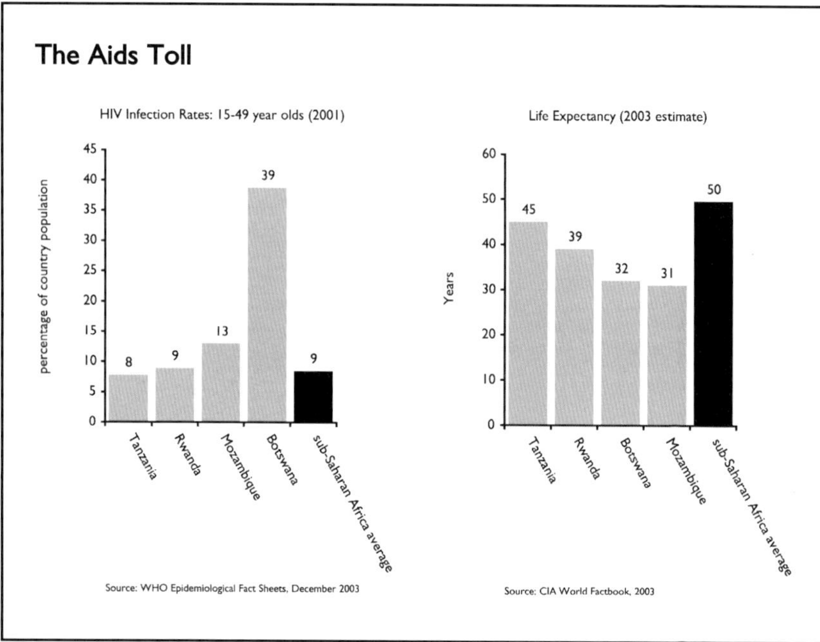

The government has made prompt, praiseworthy efforts to combat the pandemic. Billboards and television advertisements encourage safe sex, and government officials keep boxes of condoms on their desks for free distribution. The free handout of anti-retroviral drugs is being piloted, in partnership with Merck and the Bill and Melinda Gates Foundation, and the national mining company Debswana runs two hospitals and an intensive AIDS-education programme for its employees. But the anti-AIDS campaign has so far done little to change behaviour or to lift a culture of silence about the disease. Public figures do not readily admit to being HIV+. For instance, on the campus of the University of Botswana the two or three deaths notices posted each week cite TB – or even less convincingly pneumonia or a "short illness" – as the cause of death. The economic as well as social consequences of AIDS will be profound: working lives are shortening to five years or less, and forecasts that the government will lose 20% of its revenues to the pandemic by 2010 have been touted.

Nor has everybody benefited equally from economic growth. Although Botswana is a "cattle country", less than 10% of Batswana own about 50% of all cattle, and almost one in two own no cattle at all. In 2001 the bottom twenty percent of the population survived on 2.2% of national income. Four out of five rural households live on remittances from a family member in town or abroad: since migrant men and husbandless women are especially vulnerable to AIDS, this worsens a cycle of infection and poverty.

Other notable non-benefiters from diamond wealth are the Kalahari Bushmen or Basarwa, whose forcible removal from their ancestral lands sparked worldwide protests in 2002. This was the latest in a sixteen-year long series of deportations, under which Basarwa have been moved to "resettlement camps" where hunter-gathering is impossible and they become dependent on handouts and alcohol. Unproven (so far) speculation that diamond mining accounts for the removals continues to harm Botswana's reputation.

GDP growth has been ineffectual in broadening and diversifying the economy, and particularly in creating jobs. Despite government efforts, Botswana has been unable to emulate the Asian tigers in building up a large-scale competitive manufacturing base: manufac-turing still only produces 5% of GDP, compared to mining's 30-40%. As a result, employment in the formal sector remains elusive for most: unemployment is officially 21%, but unofficial estimates place it closer to 40%. A large proportion of Batswana are engaged in low-productivity activities such as hawking or subsistence farming, and what new jobs there are – in education and central government – are public-sector. Unemployment and inequality are also, it should be pointed out, the fault of the geographical distribution of the population. In many rural areas, the population is simply too small to support businesses on a scale that could make an impact on living standards. That is why most rural settlements consist of nothing more than a shop, a bottle store and perhaps a garage.

Partly to blame for Botswana's failure to diversify, paradoxically, is its diamond wealth. With diamonds on tap, governments have been able to ignore the economy's structural faults, and put off painful reforms. When the going is good (as has been largely the case ever since independence), this mode of rule can be successful. But whether the BDP can survive a prolonged economic downturn remains to be seen. Though new diamond seams are still being discovered, currently known reserves will only last about another 20 years.

On the political side, Botswana may similarly be living on borrowed time. The country's traditional culture of respect for authority is eroding, particularly amongst the young. Though the BDP is still very popular in the countryside, it is much less so in the towns, and if the opposition ever managed to unite and organise, it might give it a run for its money. The BDP, however, shows little signs of modernising in step with society. Increasingly, it shows disdain for opposing views, even from its own backbenchers. A number of laws curb press freedom, in particular 1994's Economic Crimes and Corruption Act, which restricts access to and publication of information regarding police investigations into corruption allegations, and a proposed new Mass Media Communications Bill, which will, if passed, force the registration of publications and journalists.

Out of keeping with its historic ease with foreign investment and expertise, the government has also been willing to portray organs of civil society that it is unable to control as foreign stooges. The Basarwa issue is a classic example: at the height of 2002's row, ministers accused minority-rights activists of being "racist whites" who wanted to keep the Basarwa "chasing wildlife and dressing in hides". Survival International (a London-based NGO helping the Basarwa in Botswana), was labelled a "terrorist" organisation, and their provision of satellite 'phones to the Basarwa described as "highly seditious".

Typically of the compliant and shallow-rooted third sector, the leading local native-rights charity, Ditshwanelo, swiftly distanced itself from Survival International, criticising its tactics as confrontational and "un-Botswanan". Trades unions are similarly weak, since by law trades union officials cannot be employed on a full-time basis, and strikes are only legal after a long arbitration process. Incredibly, there has never actually been a legal strike in Botswana – and this is certainly not because workers are contented. Instead, "illegal" strikes (albeit infrequently) occur, laying workers open to an over-exuberant police force not afraid to crack heads in the services of "legality" and "stability."

Conclusions

Crucial to Botswana's success has been its use of diamonds to the benefit both of elites – through programmes aimed at boosting beef production and the commercial sector – and of the general public, through the provision of infrastructure and public services. This has won the state support from all sections of the community, and given governments a "national" rather than simply a class appearance. Though rural areas remain poor, freedom from taxation and the appearance of roads, clinics and schools (all absent prior to independence) have won the post-1966 state a high degree of acceptance and legitimacy.

Botswana also, however, faces urgent challenges, in particular fairer distribution of the benefits of economic growth, and taboo-breaking management of the HIV/AIDS pandemic. Commitment to development on the part of political and bureaucratic elites is central, but not enough. This is particularly so as a new generation of Batswana emerge who do not remember how Botswana was before the country's rapid growth and development. These people are much less patient than older generations, and may well be the ground from which a credible opposition springs.

Further reading

Danevad, Andreas (1993) *Development Planning and the Importance of Democratic Institutions in Botswana* Bergen: Christian Michelsen Institute.

Du Toit, Pierre (1995) *State Building and Democracy in Southern Africa: A Comparative Study of Botswana, South Africa and Zimbabwe* Pretoria: HSRC.

Edge, Wayne and Mogopodi Lekorwe (eds.) (1998) *Botswana: Politics and Society* Pretoria: Van Schaik.

Good, Kenneth (1993) 'At the Ends of the Ladder: Radical Inequalities in Botswana', *Journal of Modern African Studies*, vol. 31, no. 2.

Harvey, Charles and Stephen Lewis (1990) *Policy Choice and Development Performance in Botswana* London: MacMillan.

Jefferis, Keith and T.F. Kelly (1999) 'Botswana: Poverty Amid Plenty', *Oxford Development Studies*, vol. 27, no. 2.

Parsons, Neil, Willie Henderson and Thomas Tlou (1995) *Seretse Khama, 1921-1980* Gaborone: Macmillan/Botswana Society.

Samatar, Abdi Ismail (1999) *An African Miracle: State and Class Leadership and Colonial Legacy in Botswana's Development* Portsmouth: Heinemann.

Stedman, Stephen John (ed.) (1993) *Botswana: The Political Economy of Democratic Development* Boulder: Lynne Rienner.

Taylor, Ian (2003) 'As Good as it Gets? Botswana's "Democratic Development"', *Journal of Contemporary African Studies*, vol. 21, no. 2, May.

Taylor, Ian and Gladys Mokhawa (2003) 'Not Forever: Botswana, Conflict Diamonds and the Bushmen', *African Affairs*, vol. 102.

Tsie, Balefi (1996) 'The Political Context of Botswana's Development Performance', *Journal of Southern African Studies*, vol. 22, no. 4, 1996.

Rwanda GDP Growth

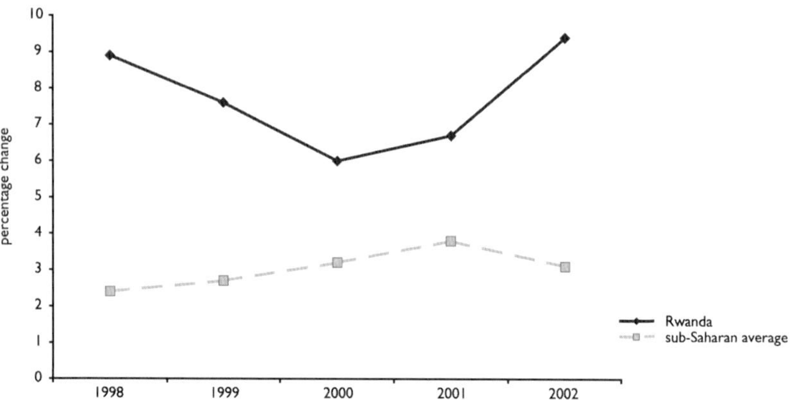

Source: IMF World Economic Outlook, September 2003

Rwanda Inflation: Consumer Price Index

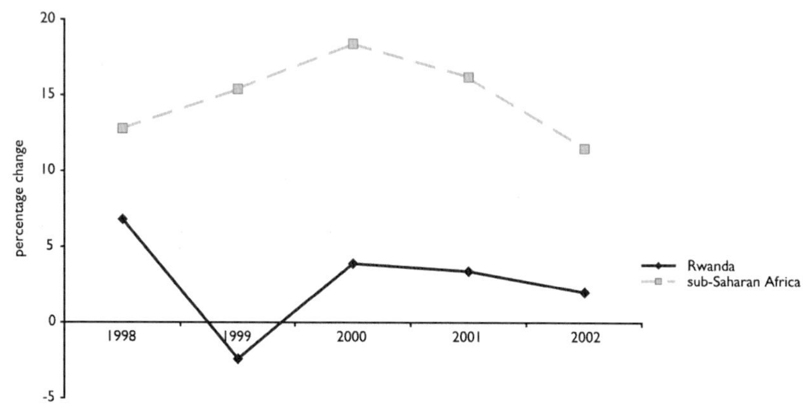

Source: IMF World Economic Outlook, September 2003

3. Rwanda

Gregory Mthembu-Salter

Rwanda is a small central African country of eight million people, packed into a land area only slightly larger than Wales. Its population density, at 300-400 people per square kilometre, is twenty times the African average. After prolonged international obscurity, the country achieved instant notoriety in 1994, when a genocide that killed somewhere between 800,000 and one million people became the continent's tragic counterpart to the stunning success of South Africa's first democratic elections. Since 1994 however, Rwandans have pulled their country back from the abyss, achieving peace, a measure of political stability, and sustained poverty-reducing economic growth. This paper examines these successes, how they have been achieved, whether they are all they seem to be, whether they will last, and whether they can be emulated.

Tutsis and Hutus

The first humans in Rwanda were Twa hunter-gatherers, joined by 1000

BC by Bantu clans practising agriculture. By 500 BC pastoralism had emerged, and by 1000 AD steadily increasing task specialisation led to the emergence of a cattle-owning class, called Tutsi. Nilotic pastoralists also migrated into the region over the next 400 years. However, the notion first propagated by colonial "experts", and later by the indigenous architects of genocide, that pastoralist Tutsis from Ethiopia invaded and subjugated an agricultural Hutu society is simply false.

By the 15th century, a Tutsi monarchy had begun an expansionist drive that it sustained until the late 19th century, when it was checked by European conquest. Germany was the first coloniser, but Belgium inherited the territory, which was linked to neighbouring Burundi, after World War I, and in 1926 incorporated both into the Belgian Congo.

The Belgian colonial authorities treated Rwanda, like its other colonies, as a forced labour camp. Rwandans were commandeered with little or no pay into public works, church construction, land irrigation, cash crop cultivation, and factory work in neighbouring Congo. Peasants were told what crops to grow, and were often required to sell them at artificially low prices. The Belgian authorities, whose view was shared by the powerful Roman Catholic Church, regarded Tutsis as inherently superior to Hutus, and born to rule them. Hutu chiefs were removed, and Tutsi chiefs allowed near total discretion in their appropriation of labour and produce from the peasantry. Unsurprisingly, many Rwandans became desperate to escape, and throughout the colonial era, migrant workers poured into Uganda seeking better pay and conditions.

In the early 1950s, under pressure from the UN, the Belgian administration reluctantly introduced limited democratic reforms. The Tutsi elite demanded immediate independence instead, so the administration switched its allegiance and supported Grégoire

Kayibanda, a Hutu catechist turned politician, who formed the Mouvement Démocratique Républicain-Parmehutu (MDR-P), advocating Hutu emancipation first, and independence later. With the connivance of the Belgians, MDR-P organised the first pogroms against Tutsis in 1959. After thousands were slaughtered by state-sponsored militia, around 300,000 other Tutsis fled as refugees to Burundi and Uganda. The MDR-P won communal elections in 1960 amid yet more Tutsi massacres, toppled the monarchy and led Rwanda into independence in 1962.

By the 1970s, Kayibanda's rule had degenerated into corruption and ineptitude, from which few but those from his hometown of Gitarama benefited. In 1973, Kayibanda was toppled by his commander-in-chief, Juvenal Habyarimana. Habyarimana's accession to the presidency was accompanied by further politically orchestrated massacres in which an estimated 100,000 mostly Tutsi people were killed.

Habyarimana established a one-party state in which Tutsi participation in public life was limited by quotas, and cultivated close relations with France, which replaced Belgium as the main source of aid and military assistance. In September 1990, and with the backing of Ugandan president Yoweri Museveni, Uganda-based Tutsi refugees called the Rwandan Patriotic Front (RPF) invaded. The RPF made substantial territorial gains, but was blocked from capturing Kigali, the capital, by French troops. Faced with military stalemate, and under pressure from donors, Habyarimana eventually consented to multiparty politics, and in 1992 formed a new government including a reconstituted MDR. The government opened negotiations with the RPF, resulting in a power-sharing agreement, signed in Arusha, Tanzania in August 1993. 2,500 UN troops were subsequently deployed to help implement the deal.

Habyarimana might have signed in Arusha, but his regime's most powerful inner-circle, the *akazu*, never accepted power-sharing, and while Habyarimana delayed the agreement's implementation, others in the *akazu* armed and trained young Hutu militia and stockpiled weapons. By April 1994, Habyarimana had run out of delaying tactics, but then, on April 6th, his plane was shot down over Kigali, killing him instantly. The next day, the *akazu* installed an interim government and launched the genocide. UN Security Council members, who had been warned for several months that a genocide was imminent, chose to misrepresent it as chaotic tribal warfare, and criminally weakened the UN force until only 270 troops, with no mandate to intervene, remained to observe the death toll mounting.

The RPF meanwhile renewed its military offensive, defeated the Forces Armées Rwandaises (FAR, the Rwandan armed forces), and took Kigali in July. The RPF advance stopped the genocide, and encouraged the return of Tutsi refugees, but precipitated the exodus of up to two million Hutus, mostly to Zaire, herded by remnants of the old regime. The Zairean refugee camps attracted international media attention, though journalists mostly failed to discern that the FAR was using the camps to regroup its forces. The new, RPF-led Rwandan government's warning that the international community must act to prevent this went unheeded, and in 1996-7 it invaded eastern Zaire and forcibly broke up the camps.

Rwanda invaded Zaire, now re-christened the Democratic Republic of Congo (DRC), for a second time in August 1998, seeking to topple president Laurent Kabila, whom it accused of assisting the ex-FAR. The Rwandan invasion was supported by Uganda but opposed by Zimbabwe and Angola, leading to a war which lasted until military stalemate and South African mediation brought it to an end in 2002.

Rwanda's aggression damaged its international standing, and led to a fall-out with Uganda, following conflict between Rwandan and Ugandan forces in the Congolese city of Kisangani during 1999-2000. The perception is widespread that Rwanda's DRC intervention was all about plunder, and certainly, Rwanda benefited from unrecorded mineral exports from the DRC. However, overall the war damaged the Rwandan economy, and more credence should be given than has been to the Rwandan government's claim that it was genuinely trying to end the threat posed by the ex-FAR.

After the genocide

Over 100,000 people have been imprisoned on suspicion of genocide since the RPF took power. Genocide trials began in 1996. However, the conventional courts lack the capacity to try everyone, so mass trials in community courts, using a remodelled version of a traditional judicial system called *gacaca*, began in 2002. Meanwhile, the International Criminal Tribunal for Rwanda (ICTR) began work in Arusha in 1995, concentrating on key genocide perpetrators. Thirteen cases have been concluded so far. The ICTR is supposed to wind up in 2008, but its chances of completing its case-load to deadline have been weakened by government opposition to its investigation of RPF war crimes.

Economic policy since 1994 has been liberal and donor-friendly, successfully capitalising on guilt-induced generosity towards Rwanda, following donor countries' dismal failure to stop the genocide. The government completed a Poverty Reduction Strategy Paper (PRSP) in 2002 which calls for real GDP growth of 5% a year, continued macroeconomic and price stability, and increased government spending on rural infrastructure and services. Following the devastation of the genocide, which saw real GDP fall 50% in a year, real GDP growth rates have been among the highest in the world. The government is serious about implementing the PRSP, though its enthusiasm for increased expenditure to finance it has worsened relations with the IMF, which demands a tighter fiscal stance.

In 2000 – following a period of political turmoil during which the parliamentary speaker fled into exile and the prime minister resigned – president Pasteur Bizimungu, the most prominent Hutu member of the predominantly Tutsi RPF, was forcibly manoeuvred by the party elite into resigning from office. Bizimungu was later imprisoned for allegedly promoting ethnic division, and remains in detention. Bizimungu was succeeded as president by Paul Kagame, who had led the RPF to victory against the FAR in 1994, and had long been considered the *de facto* leader of the country.

A new constitution was accepted overwhelmingly in a referendum in May 2003. Shortly afterwards – almost certainly at the government's instigation – the national assembly and some within the MDR requested the MDR's dissolution, which the government accepted. Following the departure from the scene of the RPF's main electoral rival, Kagame won presidential and legislative elections, held on August 25th, September 29th and October 2nd, by a landslide, with an officially declared 95% of the vote. Though EU observers judged the elections a significant democratic step forward, they also strongly criticised the government for intimidation, harassment and arrest of opponents during the campaign. The government denied the allegations.

Managing ethnic rivalry

Ethnic tensions predate colonialism in Rwanda, but only under the

Belgians were Hutu and Tutsi defined as binary opposites (Twa – now only 1% of the population – were ignored). Tragically, during the colonial era many elite Tutsis adopted the colonists' view that they belonged to a distinct and noble race. Later, the vengeful Hutu counter-elite propagated this notion of distinctiveness too, breaking with the nationalist trend of independence movements such as Julius Nyerere's and Patrice Lumumba's, and preaching that Tutsis were foreign interlopers whose yoke must be broken for Hutus – the real Rwandans – to be free. Tutsis became demonised as Hutu-despising, heartless tricksters who if given an inch would steal a mile, making it the vocation of the guardians of the "social revolution" to prevent them from ever ruling Rwanda again. This ideology predominated in Rwanda from independence to 1994. For over 30 bloody years, people in authority were promoted for believing and acting on it, and demoted for not believing it or acting on it. It is why in 1994 Habyarimana's *akazu* preferred to try and kill all Tutsis rather than allow the RPF into government. It is indeed an ideology of genocide.

The RPF says it is committed to defeating this ideology. To this end, the government refuses to negotiate with Hutu-supremacist militia, instead pursuing a no-holds-barred military offensive against them. Unsurprisingly, this has not won hearts and minds, boding ill for the future. Specifically, thanks to Rwanda's often brutal occupation during the war, Rwandans, and Tutsis in particular, are more hated in the eastern Democratic Republic of Congo than they have ever been, and anti-Rwandan government militia will probably always find a haven there. Nonetheless, the ex-FAR and its allies have been successfully prevented from gaining a toehold in Rwanda, and though fighting still rages in eastern DRC, there has been peace in Rwanda since 1998.

Although the RPF won outright military victory in 1994, it opted, wisely, to construct post-war government on the basis of the Arusha agreement, which it had signed along with most other political parties in 1993. This has had a positive effect, since the Arusha agreement is a very good one in the main, aimed at creating institutions and practices that check ethnic and regional polarisation, and steering Rwandans away from the politics of exclusion. The agreement advocates reduced presidential power, increased power for the prime minister and national assembly, and strengthened judicial independence. It forbids all requirements to disclose ethnicity, on identity cards or otherwise, and all forms of racial discrimination. It also stipulated that key ministries should be shared out between the main political parties.

The post-1994 government has done all these things, and they have all helped enormously. Yet often – too often – the implementation of Arusha (which was superseded by a new constitution this year) has been more in the letter than the spirit. For a start, the RPF took for itself all the most important government posts that had been reserved in Arusha for Habyarimana's party, the Mouvement Révolutionaire National pour le Développement (MRND). While there was no way the MRND, having just perpetrated genocide, could have joined the government, cabinet in the last nine years has been far less balanced than Arusha intended. The post of prime minister was preserved post-1994, as per the Arusha requirement. However, in practice there has been a high turnover of incumbents, none of whom ever wrested much power from the presidency, and some of whom had to flee the country after trying. Though the RPF has been a minority in the national assembly since 1994, in practice the assembly has been directed and overseen by an RPF-controlled forum of political parties with the power – often exercised – to remove parliamentarians and ministers. The forum played a key role in the RPF's recent electoral victory, by investigating and then recommending the dissolution of the MDR – the RPF's main rival – for alleged irremediable genocidal tendencies. This was despite the fact that the RPF had found itself able to cohabit with the MDR in government since 1994.

The 2003 constitution guarantees freedom of association and assembly. However, in the name of fighting the ideology of genocide, the constitution also introduces important restrictions on civil liberty. Article 14, for example, forbids "revision or negation" of the genocide. Article 34 forbids "ethnic, regional, racial or divisive" propaganda. Many Hutus believe that Tutsis dominate government, the armed forces, the judiciary, the commercial sector and academia. Whether they are right or wrong, their desire to speak out on the subject is legitimate and impossible to legislate away. Many Hutus also believe that just as there are genocide trials, there should also be trials for alleged RPF war crimes, particularly those committed in the northern provinces of Byumba and Ruhengeri during 1990-93. But those who speak out on the subject are accused of breaking the law, and labelled racist or believers in genocide. Many have been arrested and detained; some have "disappeared". This makes people frightened to talk, but it also makes them angry. Angry people are ripe for mobilisation by extremists, and this is a major long-term risk to political stability.

The presidential and legislative elections of August-October 2003 completed Rwanda's formal transition to democracy, which has many positive aspects. National elections were preceded by a series of local polls starting with the smallest units of government, so that just nine years after a genocide that topped thirty years of dictatorship, almost everyone holding public office in Rwanda has been elected, either directly or indirectly. Campaigning and voting in each poll was peaceful. Far-reaching affirmative action benefited women, young people and the disabled. Women have 24 reserved seats in the new parliament, youth councils two, and the disabled one. Seven different political parties are represented in the assembly, and several also in the new senate. President Kagame appears genuinely popular, with an enormous mandate from the electorate (ballot-rigging notwithstanding) who voted for him across ethnic lines.

Yet the irony is that this formal transition to democracy has been accompanied by a shrinking of de facto political space. After the MDR was dissolved, a moderate Kagame-supporting offshoot was allowed to form, while a more radical anti-Kagame offshoot was not. Only parties that supported Kagame during the presidential campaign won seats in the national assembly. During the presidential and legislative election campaigns, genuine opposition parties were accused of "divisionism". Campaign managers and supporters were monitored, harassed and detained, and ordinary Rwandans now appear frightened of associating with political opposition. Without the opportunity for peaceful, home-grown protest, opposition supporters may look to violence and exile to achieve their ends, and this too is a long-term threat to peace and democracy.

Living off the land

Land ownership is a nightmare in Rwanda. Land is scarce; plots are frequently too small even for subsistence purposes; and land hunger can easily turn ugly. When Tutsis were driven from their land and into exile, their land was appropriated and redistributed. During the 1994 genocide, the local authorities often promised Tutsi-owned property to whoever would kill the occupants. The genocide caused massive upheavals in land ownership, as did its aftermath, as large numbers of land-hungry Tutsi refugees returned, while two million Hutus abandoned their fields for the refugee camps of Zaire.

The easiest solution was to let the recent arrivals settle on the abandoned land, but in 1996-7 most of the Hutu refugees came back. Driven by the need to show Hutus still in exile that it was safe to return, the government ruled that recent returnees could have their land back, but those who had returned from long-term exile, who are mostly Tutsi, could not. This was a risky move for a government whose core supporters are returned Tutsi refugees, and although it helped avert civil war in the countryside, the measure prompted much outrage and bitterness. Its effect has been tempered by the fact that Hutus who participated in the genocide, or who are accused of doing so, have been imprisoned in large numbers. This is not supposed to affect their land ownership, but in practice it often does, since the temptations of empty, uncultivated fields often prove too much for neighbours.

As in many parts of the world, women have weak property rights, and can lose their land to male relatives if their husbands die. This has been a huge problem for the widows of genocide victims, and many have been summarily ejected from their properties by their male in-laws. The government has strengthened the property rights of women, and such land evictions are now less common. However, women's organisations say there is still a long way to go, and further reform is expected to be one of the major aims of women representatives in the new national assembly.

The government's long-term aim is to reduce rural population density by encouraging people into provincial towns, consolidating smallholdings to make them more viable, and creating the conditions for the emergence of a prosperous, surplus-generating farming community. Better rural services and infrastructure are important, and underway. Also vital is property-law reform, so that owners have freehold rights enabling them – de Soto style – to borrow using their land as collateral. The government knows this, yet, aware of the extreme sensitivities around the issue resulting from the turmoil of the last decade, is moving very slowly towards this goal.

The government is liberal in economic outlook, and firmly pro-trade. Rwanda becomes a fully-fledged member of the Community of Eastern and Southern Africa (Comesa) free-trade zone on January 1st 2004, when all imports of Comesa origin will attract a zero tariff. The government is lobbying hard to join the East African Community (EAC), which is also intended to reduce regional tariff barriers. Throughout all the political difficulties of the last few years with Uganda, trade between them has generally been allowed to continue unhindered. Import tariffs for goods from outside Comesa, while still high, are at least efficiently administered by the semi-autonomous Rwanda Revenue Authority (RRA).

The government understands the need to diversify the export base away from tea and coffee, for which international prices are slumped at historic lows, and from which income is insufficient to cover the import bill. According to official statistics, exports totalled only $68m in 2002, compared to $253m of imports. Even taking into account unrecorded exports of food, telecommunications and financial services, this trade gap appears uncloseably wide.

There has been substantial new investment in the country since 1994, particularly from South Africa. The South African mobile phone giant MTN has established a successful monopoly mobile phone network, though South Africa's fuel company Engen abandoned its investment in Rwanda in 2001 after its general manager received death threats. Engen's assets were subsequently taken over by a Rwandan consortium with close links to the ruling party. Disturbing as Engen's experience is, inept management was also a factor, and many foreign companies say they are very happy with the investment climate. Heineken, which runs the monopoly brewer Bralirwa, says it receives good co-operation from the government, adding that it finds the authorities honest. By contrast, many Rwandan operators report that official corruption is rife, with a few alleging that it is worse than before 1994.

The government is committed to privatisation. A private management team already runs the energy parastatal Electrogaz and it is likely that the sale of the country's tea estates will start during 2004. The telecommunications company Rwandatel is being prepared for privatisation, and the Banque Commerciale du Rwanda (BCR), the country's main commercial bank, has been recapitalised with the help of a World Bank loan, and will also, according to the finance ministry, be offered for sale in 2004.

Take me for a SAP?

Thanks to sound economic policy, good policy implementation, donor support and the considerable scope for post-genocide recovery, Rwanda has among the highest growth rates in the world. Real GDP growth averaged 13% a year from 1995-99, and though by 2000 most opportunities for catch-up growth had been exhausted, by 2002 the economy was back to better-than-'94 levels, making a positive impact on poverty. Encouragingly, recorded agricultural production grew 14.4% during 2002, following 9% growth in 2001, due to good rains and, more importantly, to productivity gains. Industrial output rose 6% a year over the same two-year period, and construction grew an annual average of 7.5%. Inflation meanwhile averaged just 2.2% during 1998-2002, partly because rising agricultural production contained food price inflation, and partly thanks to conservative monetary policy.

Despite the advances of the last few years, the Rwandan economy still has major structural imbalances, including a yawning current account deficit, and a fiscal deficit of around 8.5% of GDP. The government is dependent on donors for funds, who have mostly given generously since 1994. Due to capacity constraints, budget tracking systems are inadequate, and it is hard to find out what has been spent and how. The problem was particularly acute during the DRC war, when there was significant off-budget military expenditure, though it was well-disguised and could never be proved by donors. That said however, the quality of expenditure and the use of donor funds compares well with other African countries. The elite is not conspicuously wealthy, Kagame himself has simple tastes, those caught embezzling are generally punished and there are few "white elephant" projects in evidence. There has been a Medium Term Expenditure Framework (MTEF) since 2002, which has had a positive impact, and expenditure items prioritised in the budget, particularly for poverty reduction, are generally spent as planned.

In many African countries, the PRSP appears to be little more than a tiresome hoop through which governments must jump to access donor funds and debt relief. The Rwandan government, however, appears genuinely committed to its PRSP – a home-grown, well-considered document that identifies the main constraints to poverty-reducing growth in the country, and suggests sensible ways to overcome them. According to the PRSP, 60% of Rwandans live below the nationally-defined poverty line, (for which the main cash criterion is that a household has a total level of expenditure of less than Rwafr64,000 (US$164) per adult per year.) The PRSP presents a good case for a significant increase in government expenditure to reduce poverty, which the government hopes that donors will pay for. Some donors seem prepared to do so, but others, like the IMF, are more hostile. In 2002, the government negotiated fiscal deficit limits with the IMF as part of its Poverty Reduction and Growth Facility (PRGF) agreement. But by late 2003, partly because donors withdrew funds in protest at ballot-rigging, these targets had been exceeded, and the suspension of the PRGF is now imminent. Though the PRGF only totals $5m, because many bilateral donors tie aid to it, funds will be less in 2004 than forecast in the budget, and Rwanda will also fail to qualify for further debt relief under the Heavily Indebted Poor Countries (HIPC) agreement with and Paris Club of creditor nations.

The future

The RPA's military intervention in the Democratic Republic of Congo failed to destroy its enemies there, and the RPA's retreat in late 2002, even if it was less complete than advertised, makes it unlikely that it will ever do so. Elements within the DRC government continue to support DRC-based anti-Rwandan government militia, and there is a strong chance that the militia will strengthen their offensive capacity in the medium-term. Nonetheless, the RPA will remain far stronger than the militia, and seems unlikely to suffer military defeat in the foreseeable future.

The future of domestic ethnic relations seems more problematic. *Gacaca* will, despite its many faults, help Rwandans live with the past. Increased prosperity may also help ease the pain. But the shrinking of the public space for dissent, in the name of fighting genocide, appears set to continue, leaving alienation, resentment and anger to be expressed in coded ways. Things will seem normal on the outside, but pressure will accumulate on the inside which militants will seek to exploit, and which the government ignores at its peril.

It may be that the elite's intolerance or fear of political opposition, which underpinned the thorough curtailment of opposition parties' chances during the 2003 elections, will ease with the passing of time, and that by 2010, when the next presidential election comes round, a genuine contest will be permitted. Let us hope so. But as it is, parties other than the RPF have to tread very carefully, somehow finding ways to cultivate distinct identities without attracting accusations of "divisionism".

The Church's moral influence has been hugely compromised by the active participation of so many of its leaders in the genocide, and little can be expected of it until it takes this painful truth to heart. It has not yet done so. Yet outside the Church, civil society is weak, and many so-called civic organisations are umbilically connected to the ruling elite. There are, however, grounds for hope. Civil society may strengthen and become more independent, and may challenge the government to ease its grip. Decentralisation will probably achieve a measure of empowerment for people at local level. Representatives of women, youth and the disabled in the national assembly can perhaps play a useful role in opening up the space for civil society, and interventions by donors and international NGOs could also prove important here. But if this does not happen, and civil society remains weak and the government all-powerful and monolithic, democratic transition will have stalled.

The government now has a mandate from the voters, and is thus in a better position to attempt the difficult reforms to land ownership required to give people, and particularly women, improved security of tenure. This, at least, is government policy. Yet the government has reason to hesitate too. *Gacaca* begins in earnest in 2004, and no one knows what impact it will have in the countryside. Killers will be released to live alongside their neighbours. New evidence will emerge against many, who will suddenly be liable to arrest and a possible death sentence. This may therefore not be the ideal time to shake up land ownership. Nonetheless, the issue has to be faced at some point, and Kagame's past form suggests that he probably will tackle it during the current presidential term, pushing through reforms that strengthen individual tenure. Whether this will result in farmers being able to borrow using their property as collateral remains uncertain, for this would require a change in the outlook of Rwandan banks, which have historically never displayed much enthusiasm for lending to the poor.

The value of Rwanda's traditional exports are doomed to remain low in perpetuity. Small volumes of tea and coffee will never make the country rich, and diversifying the export base is a necessity. There are signs of this: notably sales abroad of food crops, including potatoes, and colombo-tantalite, a mineral used in the manufacture of cellphones. Mainstream agricultural exports to neighbouring states are rising as domestic production increases, though to date the increase is almost entirely unrecorded. At the same time, many domestic manufacturers fear closure in the face of increased regional competition. Services exports to neighbours look more promising, though they will probably always be mainly limited to Burundi and the DRC, and little growth can be expected in the more lucrative markets of Tanzania, Uganda and Kenya.

Although trade revenues may be diminished by the Comesa zero tariff agreement, the government is likely to stick with it, having accepted the argument that the country as a whole will benefit from free trade. The privatisation process, meanwhile, is set to continue, and will generate increased foreign investment, which will boost productivity and profitability.

The exceptionally high real GDP growth rates of the post-genocide years cannot be sustained. However, if the government sticks to its current economic policies – and the reappointment of finance minister Donald Kaberuka since the elections is a sign that it will – targeted continued real annual growth of at least 5% is possible for several years at least. Growth will be driven by improved agricultural productivity, as the benefits of continued rural recapitalisation are felt, by the growing sophistication of the services sector, and by the construction industry, which is enjoying a sustained boom. There is a good chance that with careful monetary management, inflation will remain low too, though if the government increases domestic borrowing too much it may creep higher.

The era of post-genocide goodwill from donors is fast passing. The British government is still a generous believer, and there remain other important supporters within the EU. But the IMF – a major gateway to other donor funds – is taking a much tougher line. The government has little choice, therefore, but to reach and sustain agreements with the IMF, particularly during 2004 when the budget requires keeping the PRGF, and therefore HIPC, on track. This reality is bitterly resented by the government, and negotiations will not be easy, but ultimately the government is unlikely to break with the Fund.

Conclusions

The preceding analysis suggests that the Rwandan government's approach to the transition to democracy and the management of ethnic conflict, while understandable after the traumas of the past, is closing down democratic, non-violent political space, and makes future armed conflict more likely.

The Rwandan genocide and wars have had a phenomenally far-reaching effect on sub-Saharan Africa, and it is in no government's interests for them to happen again. But the ability of Western governments to persuade the government to alter course and allow effective political opposition is tightly circumscribed. In the eyes of the Rwandan government – and indeed of any dispassionate observer – the West has proved that it will sit back and watch Rwandans slaughtered in huge numbers, entering the fray only when the bloodletting is over. Whilst this is not an argument for disengagement, the Rwandan government can never be relied on to respond positively to Western moralising on democracy and human rights, as its furious response to the EU observers' report on the 2003 election attests. African governments, and the South African government in particular, have a better chance. The Rwandan government respects the South African government immensely, and Kagame has made sure that his country is at the forefront of South African president Thabo Mbeki's brainchild, the New Economic Partnership for Africa's Development (NEPAD). NEPAD's peer review mechanism may one day be capable of prodding Rwanda in the direction of political liberalisation, but this day has not yet come. In the meantime, South African political institutions should use the many links in place between them and their Rwandan counterparts, and the goodwill that underlies them, to encourage a deeper transition to democracy.

Western donor governments have far more influence over the future direction of Rwandan economic policy. Donor pressure via the IMF during PRGF negotiations in 2002 was instrumental in encouraging the Rwandan government to pull its troops out of the DRC. However, this kind of covert political pressure can often backfire, weakening economic conditionality by encouraging recipient governments not to take it seriously. Donors' demands for peace and clean elections, though justified, would have been better made upfront and explicitly: as it is, the Rwandan government has been given good reason to treat equally important economic requirements merely as a cover

Institutions that can hold the executive in check, such as the recently established Auditor-General, should be provided with the capacity to function effectively, and donors should urge further progress, including the establishment of a genuinely independent public ombudsman. Additionally, while encouraging privatisation, donors should look for ways during the process to ensure that the rights of workers are respected. On the tea estates, for example, the right to strike is non-existent. Rwandan trade unions are weak, and cannot turn this around on their own, but if donors linked assistance to the extension of workers' economic rights, the government would soon get the message, and Rwandan workers would be the better off for it.

Most African governments are, perhaps, loathe to learn lessons from Rwanda. After all, the country is tiny, poor, has experienced the worst ethnic problems of any on a continent notorious for them, and has made a bad name for itself with its aggressive military adventures in the DRC. Yet there are important lessons to learn. For a start, Rwanda shows that a better future is always possible, even after the worst nightmares of genocide and civil war. Furthermore, on a continent plagued by chronic short-termism, Rwanda has shown that careful medium-term political thinking, translated into an achievable plan of action which the government then sticks to, can yield impressive results. The transition to this year's multiparty elections seemed impossible in 1994, and was fraught with danger, but the government approached the issue coolly, methodically, and in good time, and achieved almost exactly the outcome it intended. That might not be quite the liberal democracy others hoped for, but still, it demonstrates the Rwandan government's awesome ability to formulate and execute political strategy.

In the economic sphere, the main lesson from Rwanda's performance since 1994 is that sound economic policy formulated via a locally-owned PRSP, that takes a realistic approach to constraints but is nonetheless inspired by ambitious vision, and which is coupled with top-down dedication to good economic management, yields striking dividends. The relative lack of venality of Rwanda's ruling elite is a major bonus, of which many other governments in the region should take note. Yet the fact that despite its obvious commitment to reform, Rwanda is currently in difficulties with the IMF, sends a different message to the rest of Africa. The message is that donors only care about economics when it suits them, and that in the end getting the money is all about politics. This is the wrong message, and for the sake of Rwanda and of Africa, it needs to change.

Mozambique GDP Growth

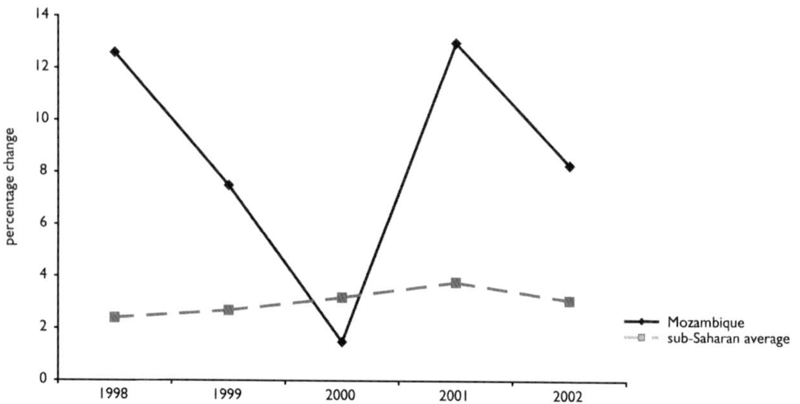

Source: IMF World Economic Outlook, September 2003

Mozambique Inflation: Consumer Price Index

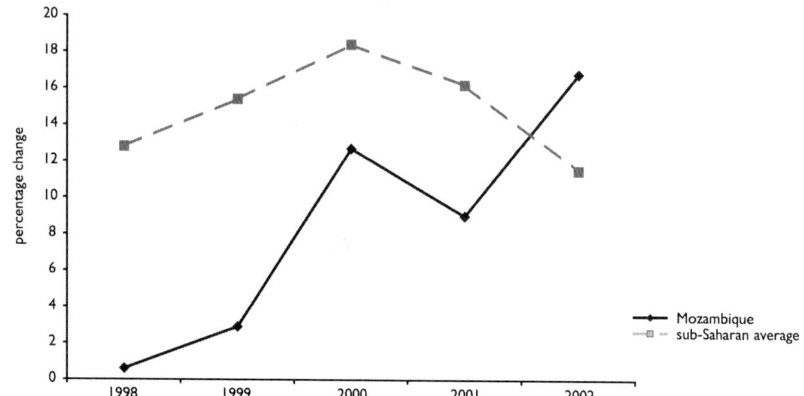

Source: IMF World Economic Outlook, September 2003

4. Mozambique

Douglas Mason

Mozambique is commonly cited as a positive example of post-conflict recovery, and as an African success story. In what respects is this so, and what, if anything, is replicable from its experience?

In the nearly ten years since elections were held at the conclusion of its civil war, Mozambique has experienced relative peace and stability. Conflict has ended, political competition is directed through elections and parliament, the institutions and forms of multi-party democracy have taken hold. Sustained, high levels of economic growth have been achieved, with average annual real GDP growth of 9% for twelve consecutive years. Substantial progress has been made in investing in the social sectors and in reducing poverty.

There are many caveats attached to the success story moniker. Progress is off a low base; growth is imbalanced; investment is concentrated in the capital and the south; grievances remain from the civil war; the ruling party uses the state to reward its supporters and exclude others; official corruption is flourishing. But the accomplishments are real and should not be minimised. Just over a decade ago Mozambique was officially listed as the world's poorest country in terms of per capita GDP (it was US$90 in 1994, against US$214 in 2002), much of the population was dependent on international food aid, and over three million people had been displaced, either abroad or internally. Fighting was still underway against the Renamo rebel – then backed by Apartheid South Africa – the one-party state was only just being abandoned, and the country was ruled by a government that had never been endorsed in an open democratic election.

Mozambique's path out of economic collapse, civil war and dictatorship holds useful lessons for other African states moving toward post-conflict recovery – Liberia, Sierra-Leone, the Democratic Republic of Congo and Angola – as well as for countries that have not experienced conflict or instability. Key to Mozambique's success has been not so much the international environment as local agency: the actions of Mozambique's main domestic actors in grasping the opportunities available to consolidate peace, and create the conditions for self-sustaining growth and development. It may be useful to separate key elements of progress into different areas: peace-making (the settlement); peace-building (national reconciliation and creation of political space); economic governance (establishing conditions for self-sustaining growth) and the situation today (a resilient but flawed democracy).

War and Peace

By the time the ruling *Frente de Libertação de Moçambique* (Frelimo) and rebel *Resistência Nacional Moçambicana* (Renamo) signed a

General Peace Agreement in Rome in 1992, Mozambique had been at war for a decade and a half, and was as wretched as any of Africa's current failed states.

The agreement was preceded by substantial shifts in the international, regional and domestic political arenas. The apartheid state in South Africa had entered its death throes, and the revanchist Portuguese ex-settler lobby had been brought to heel by the modernising Portuguese prime minister, Cavaco Silva. This left Renamo without foreign patrons and support. The Soviet Union's collapse similarly orphaned the Frelimo government, though it had already begun to open to the West and flirt with market and democratic reform following the death in 1987 of the first president, Samora Machel, and his replacement by pragmatic, sophisticated foreign minister Joaquim Chissano. A new constitution, passed in 1990, provided for multi-party democracy and separation of powers between executive, legislature and judiciary.

But ultimately, the protagonists' decision to seek peace was motivated by the understanding that outright victory was unavailable to either side. By the early 1990s Frelimo had been sapped of confidence. The compounded effects of bad economic policy, civil war and military incursions by South Africa had hastened the country toward catastrophic economic collapse. Faced with the enormity of its failed Marxist experiment, Frelimo was prepared for substantial change in order to achieve peace. Moreover, it was prepared to deal with an enemy which it – justifiably – reviled as an apartheid stooge.

Renamo could have sustained its guerrilla war for some time longer, even in the absence of the easily exploitable resources, such as diamonds or gold, that have fuelled so many other African conflicts. Students of Mozambique's 500 year-long colonial history find in the modern experience of Renamo echoes of the country's centuries-long tradition of banditry, and independent fiefdoms operating beyond the reach of weak central authorities. Already by 1992 the war had continued for some years longer than expected, as the movement rebuffed various peace overtures, and for some time it was believed that Angola would achieve peace first.

In 1992 Renamo was regarded as a primitive and volatile rebel group, a prototype for newer warlord-led bands such as the Revolutionary United Front (RUF) and West Side Boys in Sierra Leone, or Liberians United for Reconciliation and Democracy (LURD). It had neither strong leadership, capable personnel, nor even a rudimentary ideology. Moreover, it was guilty of horrendous wartime atrocities, including the mutilation of civilians, conscription of child soldiers and nihilistic destruction of public infrastructure. Faced with Frelimo, which enjoyed control of a modern state, international recognition and the advantages of nearly two decades of incumbency, it lacked the capacity and confidence to negotiate a post-war future for itself.

Several factors eventually convinced Renamo leader Afonso Dhlakama that he stood more to gain from peace than war. One was outside mediation by trusted third parties: "Tiny" Rowland of the Lonrho conglomerate (which continued to invest in Mozambican hotels and agro-businesses even at the height of the war); the San Egidio Catholic lay community; and the Italian government, which at one time provided virtually unlimited expense accounts to Renamo representatives in Rome. Self-interested or not, the effectiveness of this "trust building" – cynics would call it political bribery – was undeniable, and can be contrasted favourably with expensive, failed military peace-making efforts elsewhere, for example the multi-billion dollar UN operations in Angola, UNAVEM-I, UNAVEM-II and UNAVEM-III. Renamo was also promised a UN-administered trust fund – to which Western countries ultimately donated US$19m – to ease its transition from rebel movement to political party. Few questions were asked about its use of these funds, nor would it have been constructive to do so.

In retrospect, the Mozambican peace process, and the UN operation (UNOMOZ) that accompanied it, are regarded as among the most successful anywhere. Over 137,000 government and rebel soldiers were received at UN demobilisation camps, and provided with generous assistance to resume civilian life: starter packs of seeds and tools; shelter, food and crucially, a commitment that they would continue to receive salaries for a full two years. The UNOMOZ played a neutral role as political referee. 1994's elections took place in an atmosphere of calm, and were declared free and fair by international observers. As expected, Frelimo won presidential and legislative majorities, although the result was closer than foreseen. Renamo accepted the result, despite last-minute jitters when it threatened to pull out of the vote, alleging government vote-rigging. Decisive intervention on the part of the UN Secretary-General's representative, Aldo Ajello, and Western countries kept Renamo inside the process. Mozambique's first democratically elected government, led by Frelimo, took power, and the basis of the current post-war settlement came into being.

Central to Mozambique's success in post-conflict reconstruction and peace-building is the degree to which political space has opened up, and ethnic, regional and other conflicts have been addressed. Since the multi-party elections of '94, the forms and institutions of representative government have taken hold and shown considerable resilience. Political contest is conducted through parliament, and the rule of law, political opposition, press freedom and the independent institutions of civil society are generally respected by government. Parliamentary performance has improved, and an open, lively interface between government, legislature and media has developed – as demonstrated by ongoing revelations of bank privatisation fraud in the mid-'90s. The social and political climate has remained stable, and nascent civil society groups are becoming increasingly assertive and effective in providing services and articulating independent interests.

Serious weaknesses remain, however, and there are dissenting views on the degree to which political pluralism is genuinely flourishing. Often, only the outward forms of pluralism are tolerated, and only as long as they do not threaten Frelimo power. Opposition parties – apart from Renamo – have shown remarkable inability to develop or capitalise on opportunities over the past decade, supporting the view that civil society, despite advances, remains exceedingly weak. In practice, the most robust and effective critics of government have emerged from the middle ranks of the civil service and the ruling party itself. It was a landmark speech by a Frelimo backbencher, for example, that forced the government to abandon its attempted whitewash of the bank privatisation frauds.

Similarly, news media, though generally free from overt harassment, are not yet formidable critics of the government. The two daily newspapers (one of them government-owned), and national radio and television tamely reflect government views, and the assassination, in 2000, of a journalist investigating the bank privatisation frauds was a stark reminder of their handicaps. Three years later, bold action on the part of activists, police officers and judges resulted in the conviction of members of the hit squad that carried out the killing. However, the squad's alleged paymaster – a ne'er-do-well son of the president, Nhimpine Chissano – has not yet been arrested or charged.

Finding Renamo

When it entered into the General Peace Agreement Renamo had few illusions that it would control the next government. But it did tap into a strong sense of grievance against Frelimo and the richer south of the country, thus demonstrating a stronger claim to legitimacy than had been realised. It did surprisingly well in the 1994 elections, winning nearly 40% of the overall vote and outright majorities in five of the country's 11 provinces, including most of the heavily-populated north and centre. It maintained this support into the next elections in 1999, during which shares of the vote hardly moved.

Renamo's continuing popularity has been a source of surprise and perplexity to the international community and Frelimo, particularly so given its atrocious wartime record of human rights abuses. Moreover, it was, and remains, an extremely weak movement, lacking money, policy-making skills or any of the normative attributes of a modern political party. Instead, it remains a political force by default. Its support is "soft"; an expression of discontent with the government rather than of positive support for the other side. Nevertheless, it is possible to see in Renamo's weaknesses a reflection of its core constituency. These are the isolated and excluded populations of the north, and ambitious city-dwellers lacking the education and connections to enter the Frelimo-dominated elite.

The "fact" of Renamo reveals that Mozambique's polity is far more fractured and divided than at first appears, and that the deep wounds of the civil war have not yet healed. Although national reconciliation has been highly successful in terms of ending violent conflict, the political fault lines of the war remain, and political conflict continues. Frelimo has stuck to the letter of the peace settlement, but it has not genuinely "opened" the state or economy to outsiders.

Following the 1994 elections, Frelimo was urged by the international community to establish a unity government that would include Renamo and other independent groups. Frelimo steadfastly rejected this advice and opted to rule alone. Nor did it allow Renamo to appoint governors in the provinces where it won majorities – areas where Frelimo itself has little historical legitimacy. It also rejected Renamo's demands that it be allowed to share in state appointments, including those to public companies and joint ventures with foreign investors. As a result, it is the Frelimo elite alone that supplies a new intermediary class of political entrepreneurs.

These developments have been termed a "politics of exclusion", in that – not for the first time in Africa – a governing elite is using the state to reward supporters and marginalise opponents. Given its lacklustre showing in the last two elections, and with a third poll looming in December 2004, Frelimo may feel that it has little choice if it is to guarantee its own continuity. Despite rhetorical statements about inclusiveness, the party has made few practical concessions to achieve it, and is deeply divided on the issue. On the one hand, President Chissano and a younger, technocratic generation within government seem genuinely to be encouraging Renamo's political development and maturity, and to recognise that a volatile opposition is neither in

Frelimo's nor the country's interests. When Renamo has threatened renewed insurrection, judicious interventions by the President have kept it within legal bounds. On the other hand, large sections of the party maintain more hostile attitudes, keeping alive the memory of Renamo's wartime alliance with apartheid South Africa, and blaming it for the destruction of the socialist project. These are also the dominant attitudes of the state-owned media, in which references to Renamo are routinely prefaced with comment about its war-time abuses. In general, official objectives and attitudes are to require Renamo to recognise Frelimo's electoral victories, historical legitimacy, and unimpeded right to rule. Renamo's political defeat and marginalisation are an enduring aim.

It's grim up north

Mozambique's sprawling boundaries are the result of compromise with more powerful European states by the Portuguese colonial authorities in the late 19th century, and defy all the rational requirements of a modern nation state. They have greatly complicated the task of nation-building for independent Mozambique; problems which have been reinforced by the history of the anti-colonial struggle and post-independence development.

Frelimo was founded by Mozambique's anti-colonial intelligentsia, who were concentrated in the capital Maputo, located in the extreme south of the country. Although it eventually launched a classic guerrilla struggle in the extreme north, operating from bases in Tanzania, and now consciously seeks to be a "broad church" encompassing the entire country, it has never shaken off the perception that it is primarily a southern movement. The last three presidents have all been from the southern Shangaan ethnic group, and Chissano's designated successor as party leader, Armando Guebuza, is from Maputo. Southerners also dominate the senior levels of ministries and government agencies.

Unsurprisingly, the south still provides Frelimo's bedrock electoral support – it generally commands at least 90% of the vote there – and the party's efforts to make inroads in the rest of the country are hampered by northerners' resentment at their poorer infrastructure and services, and memories of heavy-handed rule during the post-independence period. Frelimo was a new and unknown quantity in the south and north when it took power at independence, and quickly made itself disliked with a Marxist programme to centralise economic and political authority. Its disenfranchisement of traditional leaders (regarded as tainted by contact with the Portuguese administration), and active hostility to traditional culture were also highly unpopular. Renamo, in contrast, has supported traditional authority – and is indeed itself a product of the various groups which "lost out" under Frelimo. Frelimo has since backtracked, and now courts the Catholic Church and Moslem opinion, restoring church property and attempting, controversially, to make Eid an official holiday. It has also tried to "reach out" to the populous north: all the governors appointed after the 1994 elections, for example, were originally from the provinces to which they were sent. At senior levels, however, regional administrations are disproportionately staffed, like central government, by southerners.

The north is disadvantaged economically as well as politically. According to the UN Development Programme's Human Development Index, poverty and indicators of social well-being are worst in the five provinces north of the Zambezi river, as well as the one (Tete) which straddles it. Breakdowns of budgetary spending also reveal regional concentration, with state spending per capita lower in the populous, but infrastructure-deprived, northern and central provinces.

Indicators of human development, 1998

Province	HPI*	Rank	GDP per head US$	Rank
South	39.8	–	460	-
Maputo city	21.1	1	1,340	1
Maputo province	37.3	2	174	4
Inhambane	51.7	4	170	5
Gaza	49.8	3	147	8
Centre	60.0	–	185	-
Manica	57.5	6	184	3
Sofala	55.2	5	306	2
Tete	62.1	8	158	7
Zambezia	65.3	10	126	10
North	64.3	–	159	-
Niassa	61.6	7	120	11
Cabo Delgado	67.8	11	143	9
Nampula	63.6	9	166	6
National	56.8	–	237	-

* Human poverty index (HDI), 1997 figures.
Source: UN Development Programme, Mozambique National Human Development Report 1999.

Frelimo is sensitive to regional imbalances in development and is taking some steps to address them. This is particularly so since the 1999 elections, which confirmed the regional political divisions of the first, 1994, democratic elections. The large central and northern provinces of Zambezia and Nampula are particular targets for Frelimo, and it is evident that it regards greater economic success there as both desirable and politically necessary. Public-private partnerships known as "spatial development initiatives" aim to build new infrastructure and thus attract private investment. The government is also trying to revitalise the Nacala, Sena and Beira corridor railway lines, although the last of these projects has been hampered by ongoing crisis in Zimbabwe. Tax breaks, administered by a new local development authority, promote investment in the Zambezi Valley.

Though these projects are in line with Frelimo's traditional, statist approach to development, for the most part the government has put stock in effecting economic change through its macro-economic programme and its Poverty Reduction Strategy Paper (PRSP). There is some disappointment that 10 years of double digit growth have done little for it politically. However, this is probably due to unrealistic expectations, and to the enduring strength of regional and ethnic tensions. Publicly, the party's approach to both issues is that it opposes tribalism, divisionism and threats to national unity. However, such calls have little credibility in the north and centre, where they tend to be viewed as an attempt to put a lid on justified discontent.

Getting the numbers right

Mozambique's economic performance since 1994 has been nothing short of spectacular, underpinning the country's claims to success in post-conflict reconstruction and development. Growth rates have been among the highest in the world, at an average 9% per annum despite catastrophic floods in 2000. Economic virtue and natural disaster have been rewarded with substantial inflows of foreign assistance and investment, making Mozambique one of the highest recipients of foreign capital inflows in Africa. In 2001 it was the continent's fourth-largest recipient of foreign investment, behind South Africa, Nigeria and Angola (see table). These inflows, and rising internal revenues, have enabled a doubling, in real terms, of government spending on health, education, and infrastructure, particularly roads and bridges. Rural incomes have also risen, making inroads on (still acute) poverty.

Foreign investment has been drawn to a range of sectors, including transportation, agriculture, fisheries, industry, banking and tourism. New capital-intensive industries have emerged, based on foreign mega-projects, including, inter alia, a US$2bn aluminium smelter, built by the South African-Australian conglomerate BHP-Billiton. The end of the civil war also provided opportunities for rapid catch-up growth in established sectors – such as ports and railway transportation to the countries of the interior – as well as the return and resettlement of some 3m internally and externally displaced people. Historic economic links to South Africa – disrupted by the upheavals of independence in 1975 and hostility from the apartheid regime – were restored quickly.

Private direct investment inflows to sub-Saharan Africa (US$m)

	1996	1997	1998	1999	2000	2001	Total
South Africa	816	3,811	550	1,503	969	7,162	14,811
Nigeria	1,593	1,539	1,051	1,005	930	1,104	7,222
Angola	180	412	1,114	2,471	879	1,119	6,175
Côte d'Ivoire	269	415	380	324	235	246	1,869
Mozambique	72	64	213	382	139	480	1,350
Lesotho	287	268	265	163	118	117	1,218
Tanzania	150	158	172	183	194	224	1,081
Total sub-Saharan Africa	4,340	8,135	6,520	8,095	6,079	12,789	45,958

Sources: IMF, International Financial Statistics; UN Conference on Trade and Development, World Investment Report 2002.

With minimum levels of political and economic stability, post-conflict economies in Africa can generally expect relatively robust GDP growth, of roughly 5% or more for several years. How has Mozambique managed to exceed expectations?

Two obvious, mutually reinforcing factors are responsible. The Mozambican authorities have demonstrated sustained commitment to economic reform, establishing an enabling environment for growth and development, while foreign donors, supporting success, have poured in resources. Mozambique, is in other words, an example of the virtues of a consistently-applied and generously-funded structural adjustment programme.

The Mozambican authorities have been experimenting with market reforms since their first, IMF-sponsored structural adjustment programme of 1987, and have developed close relations with – if not dependence on – donors. The programme slipped briefly in 1995, when the government lost control of monetary policy, and inflation rose. Food riots broke out in Maputo, and the IMF threatened to declare its programme "off track", provoking an unprecedented protest from bilateral donors. Having been brought back under control in the second half of the '90s, inflation spiked again in 2000 and 2001, thanks to the floods and a banking crises, but is expected to fall back to 10% in 2003.

In general, however, the government has observed strong economic discipline, providing the necessary conditions for strong economic growth, which accelerated from 4.3% in 1995 to 11.1% in 1997, dipped with the floods, but has since recovered well. Political and economic stability, an enabling environment for private sector investment, and large inflows of aid in the form of assistance for reintegration, have established a virtuous circle, allowing Mozambique to move from relief to reintegration, and from reconstruction to development.

On the political side, high-level commitment to reform has long been apparent, and key cabinet portfolios are entrusted to competent technocrats. Policy "ownership" has been strong, in particular the current Poverty Reduction Strategy, whose main tenets – high growth; quantitative and qualitative increases in delivery of social services; private sector development – are routinely referred to by Frelimo politicians. Political factors include a strong tradition of cohesion and unity within the party, and the ability to coalesce around the execution of key goals. Even the more traditionally-minded old guard have managed to find continuity in the current focus on poverty reduction with the socialist goals of the first decade of independence.

Positive results encouraged increased aid from donors eager to find and fund success in Africa. Mozambique has long held the capacity to capture the popular imagination, moving seamlessly from darling of the left in the 1970s and '80s to darling of the right in the '90s. For nearly two decades it has been one of the largest recipients of international aid in the world, with aid accounting for over half of all government spending. A key factor is donors' confidence that Mozambique has the policy framework, the political will and the institutional resources to spend the money for good – on poverty reduction; and effectively – without undue fraud or wastage. However, donors also recognise that aid dependency is not desirable, and that the government must fund an increasing portion of its own costs from domestic resources – something which it is now beginning to do.

Land and the law

All land is owned by the state in Mozambique, and this is enshrined in the 1990 constitution. However, land can be leased for long periods and individuals are allowed to own buildings and other infrastructure. A new land law was introduced in 1997 that codified these changes as well as the land rights of communities, although provisions strengthening the latter were watered down at the insistence of Frelimo hard-liners.

The lack of a functioning land market in Mozambique is a major constraint on development and economic activity. Existing regulations grant wide administrative powers with regard to land rights, contributing to rent-seeking activity by Frelimo functionaries and the politically connected. (Land law, it has been said, is "Frelimo's pensions policy.") This includes urban land, where enormous wealth was captured by the state elite when public housing was gradually sold off at nominal values. Rental income is a source of enormous wealth, particularly in the capital Maputo, as foreign agencies are not allowed to own property. Bureaucratic confusion, and a general lack of transparency and predictability in land issues, add to the expense and time involved in renting factory or office space. But although all this has negative consequences for industrial growth, the politics of land ownership give Frelimo a strong incentive to preserve the status quo, regardless of missed economic opportunities. When the minister for agriculture, Helder Muteia, spoke out in favour of land privatisation he fatally damaged his chances of succeeding Chissano as party leader, losing out to old-guard rival Guebeza.

Judicial independence is enshrined in Mozambique's constitution, as well as the presumption of defendants' innocence. Such rights were key gains of the 1990 constitution, and the past decade has seen expanded effort by the authorities to ensure the observation of basic rights and freedoms. However, practical progress is limited by incapacity and bottlenecks in weak state institutions. The judicial system is in a state of crisis, suffering from a dearth of qualified legal personnel and clogged with an enormous backlog of court cases. The authorities are aware of the extent of the problem, and are increasing the resources devoted to the system. Irregular influence in the court system is also apparent, although press, parliament and civil society are increasingly bold in exposing such abuses.

Red tape and brown envelopes

Although the strength and durability of current successes should not be under-estimated, neither should weaknesses and challenges. Regulatory tangle, bureaucratic obstruction and official corruption are all serious constraints to doing business in Mozambique, both for donors and private investors.

Human resource capacity is extremely weak, and labour shortages, particularly of skilled managerial staff, have opened up. Despite progressive salary rises in the public sector, the government often loses out to the private sector in the competition to attract and keep talent. Labour laws, drawing on socialist regulation from the 1970s, make it almost impossible to dismiss underperforming employees, and employees often abuse them, pushing up staff costs. The Ministry of Labour is commonly accused of serving no useful purpose other than the extraction of bribes – via token health and safety inspections – from foreign businesses and aid agencies. Corruption is not, however, sufficiently systematised to provide predictable protection in return. New labour legislation, prompted by rising nationalist sentiment, is also making it harder to hire expatriates.

More seriously, a two-speed economy has emerged, with divergence between poorly performing traditional sectors and dynamic modern ones. The latter, such as the multi-billion dollar aluminium smelter, are highly capital, not labour, -intensive, have few links to the broader economy and make little impact on poverty. Nonetheless, there is no evidence that these dynamic sectors are crowding out other growth and, if nothing else, they do at least boost local tax revenues and export earnings.

Mozambique's weak institutional capacity is also emerging as a key constraint. To date, poverty reduction has been driven by large, sustained increases in public spending on key areas such as primary health and education. However, recent reviews, by the government and the IMF, of performance under the Poverty Reduction Strategy reveal that the quality of public spending is poor, and has not produced adequate results. This suggests that the easy progress of the past decade, based on constant rises in spending, cannot be sustained. Instead, Mozambique must get to grips with the far more complex task of achieving institutional efficiency. Given its weak human resources this will be no easy task.

Finally, it is apparent that many of the "easy options" for economic growth available in the first decade of peace have been expended. These include the catch-up growth of post-war reconstruction, and probably also large-scale foreign direct investment, which is unlikely to continue at its current rate. Today's mega-projects are essentially one-offs, and once those already in the pipeline are complete, growth arising from them will tail off. This points to a far harder struggle; that of improving performance in near-stagnant but poverty-reducing traditional businesses, such as peasant-based cash cropping. The state also needs to kick-start new, labour-intensive, export-oriented sectors such as textile manufacturing. Here again, the record is not encouraging. Mozambique is a high cost economy with poor infrastructure, a weak domestic private sector and an extremely unpredictable business operating environment. Although on paper, regulation is generally adequate, any investor can attest that getting things done is slow and expensive, with no assurances of a successful outcome. Mozambique will have to try harder if it wishes to compete with the other countries of the region and sustain its current high rates of growth.

Conclusions

Mozambique's experience in crafting an enduring settlement to civil war and promoting reconstruction represents one of the most important successes of any country attempting post-war rehabilitation and development. Available opportunities were capitalised on and conditions of political and economic stability created, sufficient to spark endogenous growth and a large-scale inflow of foreign resources. Politically, an entrenched party was able to take the pragmatic decisions necessary to compromise with a despised enemy, and deliver the country from civil war. Important gains have been made in terms of national reconciliation and creating political space for the growth of civil society and independent initiatives.

Deep political fault lines remain, however, and on closer examination it is apparent that much unfinished business remains from the civil war. Frelimo is aware of these issues, although its strategy is essentially to co-opt dissent, making itself available to excluded groups as a career ladder, rather than to create a genuinely open political environment. Indeed, given its visceral belief in its own legitimacy, it is hard not to believe that it will win the December 2004 elections by whatever means necessary. This points to continued political conflict, and to the erosion rather than expansion of basic liberties.

There is also evidence that the high point of national reconciliation with Renamo and the disaffected groups it purports to represent has already been reached. The need to placate Renamo, and anchor it firmly in the democratic process, was central to the enlightened self-interest of now outgoing President Chissano. That included the understanding that Frelimo needed to encourage political development and maturity inside Renamo. But on current evidence, this is not the approach likely to be taken by Chissano's chosen successor, Armando Guebuza, when Chissano steps down after the next election. Guebuza's instincts and vision – of a Frelimo that enjoys unimpeded right to rule – appeal to the more hard-line sentiments of the party, and do not favour further national reconciliation.

On the economic side, success is to the credit of strong local commitment to implementing economic policies developed in collaboration with the IMF and World Bank. Macro-economic stability proved to be a sufficient condition to set the stage for growth, and gave donors confidence that their monies would be spent effectively.

Mozambique has also managed to neutralise the most dysfunctional elements of African political economy. Simply put, the overriding imperative of any ruling party in Africa is to achieve political and economic hegemony and satisfy urban elites, utilising the state and the resources derived from international recognition to entrench its position. Large-scale extraction of state resources is, however, fundamentally incompatible with macro-economic stability, transparency, free markets, foreign investment and poverty reduction. This "dialectic of extraction" tends to explain why governments continue to subvert reforms or pursue dysfunctional policy in the face of economic failure. One need look no further than the 30 year economic decline of Mobutu's Zaire, or Kenya under Daniel arap Moi over the past decade, for examples of the phenomenon.

Mozambique is not entirely free of the phenomenon either, and there is ample evidence that the Frelimo elite frequently abuses its political dominance to capture new areas of economic accumulation, intermediating foreign investment and aid to suit its own ends. Most spectacularly, two state-owned banks, Banco Comercial de Mozambique and Banco Austral, were plundered prior to privatisation, resulting in bankruptcy and a government-led bailout that cost the public the equivalent of 4% of national GDP. However, the political genius of the Mozambican experience has been to balance Frelimo's own political imperatives with the objectives of macro-economic stability, indicating that the authorities learned the lesson that if you get economic governance right, donors will forgive much else.

It is possible that Mozambique's greatest economic successes are already behind it. The easy growth options have already been grabbed, and further progress in the coming years will be harder to achieve. It must tackle, in other words, the problems of being a normal African country. Considering where it was a decade ago, however, this very normality is an enormous accomplishment. A final, cautionary, note is also in order on the expectations of the foreign donors, academics and well-wishers who project their own hopes onto countries that have their own historical momentum.

Despite enthusiasm for African success stories, external parties should probably accept that at some point they are going to be disappointed.